CHURCH PLANTING

THE NEXT GENERATION

Introducing the Century 21 Church Planting System

Light and **Life** PRESS

Indianapolis

KEVIN W. MANNOIA

CHURCH PLANTING THE NEXT GENERATION —
INTRODUCING THE CENTURY 21 CHURCH PLANTING SYSTEM

by Kevin W. Mannoia

ISBN 0-89367-183-5

© 1994, 1995, 1996 by
Light and Life Press
Indianapolis, IN 46253-5002
Printed in the U.S.A.

CONTENTS

FOREWORD

As one who develops reproducible systems for comprehensive regional and national strategies for church multiplication, I applaud the emergence of a new breed of leadership for the church. Kevin Mannoia is one of a growing number of denominational executives who are beginning to develop a more intentional approach to cultivate church health, growth and multiplication.

My relationship with Kevin began when he brought a team of people to our New Church Incubator training conference in October 1991. As I interacted with him, I was particularly impressed with his leadership effectiveness as a denominational supervisor of pastors and churches. Kevin has a clear sense of vision coupled with a commitment to process change responsibly. He also selects strong and catalytic leaders, then empowers and releases them to carry out their God-given mission.

As our relationship has grown, I've appreciated Kevin's willingness to take risks and invest in pilot projects. For example, the Free Methodists provided a grant to Church Resource Ministries (CRM) to develop the Parent Church Network. Kevin also played an instrumental role in bringing other denominational leaders together in the planning process for the Profile Assessment system.

A reproducible systems approach for church health, growth and multiplication must include at least four essentials: 1) Leadership development and selection; 2) Coaching systems and resourcing; 3) Multiplication of congregations; 4) Increasing existing church effectiveness.

The specific methods used must be contextualized to your own situation.

Written as a combination of a case study of what has happened and a proposal of what can happen, the Century 21 System builds on the work of others. In this seminal work, Kevin begins to articulate what it would mean for a district to embrace a reproducible systems approach for church growth and multiplication.

Although it is sometimes risky to write a book before all aspects of the content have been proven in experience, the material you'll find here will help stimulate your thinking to discover a more intentional reproducible approach within your district or region. May the Lord bless you as you seek to apply these principles.

Dr. Robert E. Logan
June 1994

ACKNOWLEDGMENTS

To the glory of God and God alone.

As this very book demonstrates, teaming in leadership is the paradigm of the next generation.

Strategic mobilizers acting in coordination and cooperation will usher the church into a highly synergistic, mission-driven era.

The hard work of many expert church leaders has provided the fabric out of which this work is woven. I give proper credit as various components are described. However, I want to acknowledge the efforts and influence of a few special contributors to this project done entirely for the building of God's kingdom.

The Reverend Steve Fitch has been invaluable in his role as assistant to the superintendent for church planting. As such he has not only extended my ministry immeasurably but provided constant direct oversight and focus to our planting enterprise. He is a rising church planting strategist. Beyond that, his encouragement, advice and feedback have sharpened the focus of this work and the ministry efforts in our area. He is a partner in ministry and a true friend. Thank you, Steve.

As you will notice throughout this work, the name *Bob Logan* appears regularly and often. Dr. Logan has had significant influence on my thoughts, strategy and work. He rightfully holds the honor of being the leading resource on church planting in America. His input has dramatically affected our effort in becoming a church planting movement. Our regular times together have allowed not only a stimulating exchange of ideas but an ongoing friendship. Thank you, Bob.

Less visible but vitally important has been the general affirmation in mission from the close advisors who constitute my cabinet. The Reverend Denny Wayman, assistant superintendent and pastor, Dr. Hank Bode, vice president of Azusa Pacific University, and Dr. Bill McKinney, public school administrator. The common mind and strong relationship among us have created an atmosphere of confidence in developing new paradigms of district ministry. Thank you, friends.

I don't know of any writer who doesn't understand the incredible contribution of those who take the patchwork of scribbles, blocks, drawings and loose pages and transform them into a surprisingly coherent, well ordered document. I am no exception. I am constantly amazed at the efficiency and speed with which work moves from Esther Hopper's desk back to mine in completed form. As my secretary and office manager, she truly provides a ministry to our district and to me. Thank you, Esther.

As a regular newspaper editor in Redlands, CA, LeOra Mudge graciously used her talents to smooth out many of the rough spots in my writing. Thank you, LeOra.

As you might expect, my family deserves a word — not necessarily for the insight my two year old might have provided on the subject, but for allowing me to take the time I might otherwise have spent on the floor, in the yard, or on the bikes. Thank you, loved ones.

And most important I acknowledge the role of my pastors in Southern California — the best. They have allowed God to fill them with such enthusiasm for church planting that the environment of this district is more conducive to big dreams than anywhere I know. Thank you, fellow servants of God.

Kevin W. Mannoia

To Kathleen, whom I love.
And to
Kristyn,
Christopher
and Corey,
a reminder
of the joy of new life.

INTRODUCTION

"It wasn't a strategic, intentional plan. It was more like a gradual realization of how individual parts should be networked and integrated to form a whole new movement in the body designed to start new churches."

That's the answer I gave to someone who asked how the Century 21 Church Planting System came to be. It actually grew out of an uneasy sense that we seemed to be basing our church planting successes on two delicate assumptions: 1) the ability of the regional leader to create momentum for church planting and 2) a group of as-yet-unknown variables that we hoped would somehow come together in just the right amounts and at just the right time to form a successful venture. In our district case we had a 35 percent chance that a new start would succeed. We didn't know it then but that's what it proved to be.

The haunting questions persist in the minds of district overseers and church growth leaders. How can we improve our chances for a successful plant? How can we prevent hurt to good-hearted, well-intentioned planters who are damaged or destroyed by a failed attempt to plant? How can we learn from our successes and failures for greater effectiveness in the future?

As our team sat through our first New Church Incubator training seminar, the proactive questions began to form themselves into an ordered pattern. Over the next six months the answers also began to fall into a system that made sense, was workable and was consistent with the overall mission of being a relationally based movement. The key factors are that planting churches must be 1) intentional and 2) systemic. That is, it must be an intentional decision and be woven into the very fabric of the ecclesiastical institution. It must not simply become a "tacked on" fad demanding a tolerant nod from leaders to appease guilt. Also, it cannot be based solely on the level of commitment, ability or competence of the district leader who happens to be in office. A church planting movement must transcend the personality of the district overseer; he will come and go; this mission must remain intact.

And so Century 21 Church Planting is a system that invades existing structures and modifies the priorities of institutions to reposition the district as a church planting movement. It's like a bookshelf that organizes resources developed independently by qualified experts. These individual "books" allow the bookshelf to integrate them into a cooperative and ordered system to help district growth. It begins not as a program to be implemented but as an attitude to be adopted; not as a package to be sold but as a fire to be kindled. It need not be fully operational before planners will see benefit because movement, any movement, is energy that can be channeled and guided by the Holy Spirit to accomplish His mission for the church.

CHAPTER 1 –
MISSION

It is my firm conviction that the church has a clear mission from God: To Make Him Known. Although it is often muddled and obscured, the mission remains the same. It awaits discovery or rediscovery by those who are charged with leadership and influence on a regional level. District overseers, pastors and key growth-minded leaders have a special need to keep the mission clear.

Often in the compartmentalization process of our institutions we assume that those on the church growth committee will "do church growth." As a result, a large segment of our most capable leaders abdicate their role of keeping the district focused on mission priorities. They have become so specialized in their thinking that they assume no responsibility for church planting. The attitude is: "My ministry is finance; Joe's responsible for growth." Such compartmentalization fractures the very soul of the church by reframing the mission. The rationale is that specialists keep only to their specialty. And so, assuming that someone else is doing it, commitment to the mission gets lost in the more urgent cogs of institutional self-preservation.

In compartmentalizing our ecclesiology we force an egocentrism onto those holding the positions. Because they become less emotionally connected with other agendas in the regional church, they develop a lop-sided passion for their own. Because they have only one agenda on their minds the tendency is to develop that agenda beyond what is necessary. The church and its mission are redefined from one narrow perspective with all other functions being subservient. And so the "legal" people have difficulty understanding why the "church planting" people don't see their work as top priority. A check and balance system results in which division and relational breakdown can distract the entire district.

It's not something unusual. It happens all the time. It's a natural process that we have allowed to happen to ourselves. When met with the overwhelming task of simply maintaining the structure, even the most well-meaning leaders and committee members get side-tracked. Their vision is confined by the paradigms from which they operate. Stephen Covey, in his book *Seven Habits of Highly Effective People,* takes great care to describe the power of paradigms. Paradigms are maps. Attitude and hard work mean nothing in achieving a goal or finding a destination if we're using the wrong map or only a small portion of it. Potential leaders absorbed in the maintenance of efficient bureaucracy are conditioned by a paradigm that is limited to one "compartment" of the whole and void of mission.

As Covey asks, "What good would a map of Detroit be to you if you're lost in Chicago?" Likewise, what good does the finance committee of your district do in achieving the mission if their "map" is one of "financial security" not "making God known"?

In reality, synergy in mission is our collective goal. Individual "compartments" or committees must adopt a new paradigm wherein their very identity is defined relative to the greater mission. Each committee understands the holistic and integrated nature of the total institution. Rather than territorial competition, all segments begin to pull together for the common, mission-driven good.

While it may require a high degree of patience and understanding to allow for these paradigms to shift, the result is cohesive, synergistic body-life. Even in the transition, we must continue to remind ourselves (all of us) that our mission is simple — to make God known.

Our district has a conference center located at about 5,500 feet elevation in the San Bernardino Mountains of southern California. The road to Oak Glen has many hairpin turns. There's one blind curve to the right, which is my favorite. Often as I travel there to retreats I take a risk and swing across the oncoming lane (which gives my wife pause). I stop on the shoulder to admire the beautiful view of the valley. Nights are especially attractive as I admire the millions of twinkling lights below. Again, I cross the descending lane and continue to the peaceful, comfort of our cabin and the warmth of Christian speakers and fellowship. In the warm cocoon of that beautiful Christian retreat, I often think of the lights in the valley below. For every one of those lights there are three or four lives that are breaking, marriages failing, murders committed, children abused, minds tortured with drugs, infants aborted.

God is calling His body, the church, to come off the mountain of our own comfort zone and enter the valley where the battle is hot. You see, He wants us to declare His kingdom to the world. What is the kingdom of God? My undergraduate religion professor, Harry Anderson, always taught: "The kingdom of God is the rule of Christ in the hearts of people." If that's the Kingdom and if expanding His kingdom is our mission, then our task is clear — to declare Christ to the broken people in the valley. Sure, it means leaving the security of our comfort zones. Sure, it means taking risks. Sure, it means getting hurt and even, at times, failing. But our mission is in the valley of hurting people where the Enemy is in heated battle. It's not on the mountain top where we retreat into the security of our own institutional, protective sub-culture.

The Dead Sea is dead because it's not flowing into anything. Species die because they don't reproduce. Seeds rot if they are not planted. Churches and districts stagnate if there is no new life. Inherent within a district are the seeds of its own reproduction — its churches. Church planting is to the larger district what new converts are to individual churches. Without them we become self-serving, self-perpetuating, self-centered flatliners. If there is to be life, there must be reproduction — of disciples and of churches. It keeps us growing, it keeps us effective, it keeps us on mission.

It is risky. We might fail or even be criticized. It may require that other issues be neglected. Of course that may prove to be good as we discover that much of what has occupied our efforts may simply turn out to be secondary attachments. It takes risk to keep the mission paramount — to witness for Christ and to plant new churches. Yet if we are serious about growth and making Him known, there is no more effective way to do so than to start new churches.

In one district of 40 churches, five are under 10 years of age. These five churches represent 12.5 percent of the churches in the district. Twenty-five percent of those in worship on Sunday morning are in those five churches. Thirty percent of those professing new faith in Christ are in those five churches. Twenty-seven percent of those moving toward full-time ministry are in those five churches. If the church plants were not considered in the overall growth of the district, the picture would be drastically different. As you can see from the example below (Figure 1), which describes this one district, church planting is the life-blood of our future.

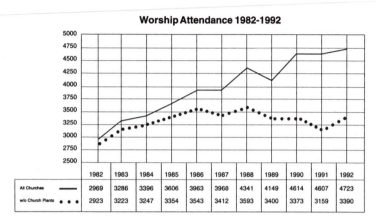

Worship Attendance 1982-1992

		1982	1983	1984	1985	1986	1987	1988	1989	1990	1991	1992
All Churches	—	2969	3286	3396	3606	3963	3968	4341	4149	4614	4607	4723
w/o Church Plants	• • •	2923	3223	3247	3354	3543	3412	3593	3400	3373	3159	3390

Figure 1

The sharp decrease in 1989 was due primarily to a pastoral failure at a large, high-profile church. While issues of leadership development are not the focus of this book, they are vital to the district pastoral team. I'll touch on it later under separate cover and develop the connection between a leader's identity and performance.

As a result of these planting successes, district morale is high. A celebrative sense of victory and confidence pervades because the mission is being fulfilled. There is no question that as denominations and districts peel away the layers of "institutional stuff" and rediscover their mission, they will be convinced that church planting is as much a part of fulfilling their mission as it was to St. Paul who went from city to city expanding the influence of Christ through church planting.

CHAPTER 2 –
LEADERSHIP

The church rises and falls on leadership. John Maxwell says, "Leadership is everything." Ninety percent of what happens in the church is attributable to leadership. Priorities of strategic implementation are determined by leadership. Atmosphere and context are controlled by leadership. When I use the term "leadership," however, I use it in a rather narrow spread. It includes bishops or general superintendents, district overseers or superintendents and pastors. Of course many lay and clergy persons who are not in these roles exert leadership influence as well. But if the persons endowed with both the gifts and position are not in full and enthusiastic support of church planting, it won't happen. Yes, these people must lead the way. Not necessarily in methods and techniques, but in priority. They certainly will not become the experts in the field. They shouldn't, because their leadership platform must be broader than planting churches. However, these leaders must lead the way in declaring the priority, developing the momentum and dismantling the obstacles.

Not long ago I sat in on a business session where ministers and lay leaders were gathered to do the business of the district. An issue of funding church planting was before the group. Many opinions were expressed by pure-hearted, sincere lay persons and ministers. Each of them had something to say that reflected their particular interest or experience. Business people were extolling the virtues of a "business-like" approach to the task. The financial experts were urging reappropriation of the funds to make the district more financially secure. The old-timers were anxious because the idea hadn't come through the right committees. Former leaders were somberly predicting failure since "we already tried that." Younger ones were frustrated with the feet dragging and were pleading to "exercise faith."

Noticeably absent was the voice of the designated leader, who, though he was not skilled in the field, had the position of overseer. Yet he failed to proclaim the priority to his people. He had for too long neglected the painstaking process of building momentum, and he refused to roll up his sleeves and work with the experts to deal with the obstacles. When the critical institutional moment came, he was caught flat-footed with nothing to say. Assuming it was normal for the committees to battle it out, he could only stand by and watch. He had nowhere to connect and no base of power with which to influence the decisions. More important he could not positively hold the cohesiveness of the group. Differing opinions lead to accusations, to anger, to division, to low morale, to frustration and to paralysis.

Leadership is not called upon for expertise but for priorities and unity in mission. No institutional group or organization will be able to articulate mission, much less fulfill it, without leadership. The leader may not be able to answer the technical questions. But he or she must be able to call the district to mission. It doesn't simply happen through sermons and reports. It happens by working with the people and constantly tying the issues to mission. Every circumstance can be a teaching moment to drive home the mission.

So, leader, unless you are prepared to assume the responsibility and commit yourself to the risk with full and enthusiastic support, don't even think about regional church planting. It may only divide your people. Even considering church planting on a district or regional level will force you to a significant paradigm shift in leadership.

Historically, the district structure has been the epitome of mid-level bureaucracy. A plethora of boards and committees exist to "keep the work going." It is best described as a committee-led organization. Committees are called upon to set priorities, purpose and mission. They are empowered to manage all programs. They must approve all actions of the district. Often this micro-managing by committee is not intentional but a direct result of leadership. Leaders assume the role of manager and abdicate authority to the committee. Perhaps it's out of fear of leadership or perhaps ignorance. The leader may simply assume that's the best way since "that's the way it's always been." The leader is relegated to a titular position focusing on paperwork, reports and committee work. Because there is no mission, no vision, no movement, the leader must justify his or her role through these secondary activities. It is "holding the form but denying the power" of leadership.

We must hasten the transition already underway from being committee-led to being staff-led and lay-driven. That is to say, leaders must step forward in vision-casting, mission articulation and priority setting. This will do more to empower lay leaders to fulfill their task on committees than anything else. Certainly committees will remain. However, they will have a foundation, a centerpoint, a platform from which to act. Let me offer a little clue to this type of leadership. While the skills necessary for assuming this type of role may be acquired, the content of what you represent may not. Notice I said "what you represent." That's because the priorities, mission and purpose of your district will largely be determined by your own. This is something that must come from within you, hammered out with God and consistent with who you are.

Leadership is not entirely a matter of management; it is projecting your priorities. Eventually, your organization will become a reflection of you. So, leader, begin by asking God, "What role do I play in Your kingdom?" "What abilities am I to deploy for Your agenda?" "What fuels my passion?" "What priorities am I to represent?" You are a leader not so much for what you can do as for who you are. If you have carefully tended the well of your own identity, you will clearly understand the equipment God has given you to project your identity into reality. Your equipment includes your gifts, your call and your personality. Actions, attitudes and priorities will naturally flow through these from a confident sense of being. They will imprint themselves upon the institution entrusted to your care. Ultimately your district will become a reflection of who you are in nature and priorities.

If your priorities do not include church planting, don't do it. But ask yourself whether someone else should be where you are in order to do it. Remember, our mission is to make God known. If your passion is not for lost people, consider where you could fit to be in step with your passion. Or ask God to give it to you. If your gifts do not equip you for district leadership, step aside. Or let yourself be developed to continue. In any case, as the leader goes, so goes the district.

If the leader is growth-minded and committed to expanding the Kingdom through church planting, the district will follow suit and become like minded.

Conversely, if the leader is by his or her actions more interested in the maintenance of the institution and status quo, then the district will find itself growing in its committee structures and bureaucracies but not accomplishing much in terms of mission. If you are a district leader, don't feel as though you need to have all the details of a plan clearly articulated and in print before making the initial commitment to mission and growth. Plenty of people and resources are available to assist you with implementing your growth-minded vision.

First and foremost you must be willing to allow growth through church planting to become an integral part of your vision and attitude in your work. Everything you do should be infected by enthusiasm and a commitment to church planting. Obviously many things for which an overseer is responsible cannot be left unattended. Crises arise that demand immediate and total attention. These additional responsibilities and urgent matters underscore the need for developing a district system that can continue the process of starting new churches even when the primary leader is forced to devote his or her attention to other pressing matters. There can be no equivocation, however, on the clear and high profile commitment of the leader to church planting. This cannot simply be a nod of intellectual assent to the concept and theory of church planting. It must be an emotional and attitudinal commitment to the mission of expanding the Kingdom through the most successful means yet discovered — beginning new churches.

There is no easy way for the district leader to come to this level of involvement and ownership. It demands intense personal scrutiny, prayer, understanding of the church in its broadest sense, capturing the vision of God for His work and hammering out a pragmatic philosophy of ministry that incorporates the starting of new churches at its very core.

One of the most effective ways to come to this commitment is through observing new churches that have experienced great success. Exposing yourself to a successful church plant and its pastor can open new horizons of possibility in your own thinking. We must believe and trust in the inherent call of God to become the foundation for the enthusiasm you may capture from a successful church plant. God has put within you the flame of desire to see His kingdom expand. Exposure to those circumstances and people that have found growth to be a reality can kindle a fire of passion within you.

Thus, for the district leader who is giving serious consideration to leading his or her group of churches in becoming a church planting movement, I suggest the following steps of preparation and confirmation:

1. Commit yourself to a significant season of prayer. A month at minimum and perhaps as long as a year may be required in constant and intentional openness before God. Ask Him to give you an open heart and mind to the specific mission-driven agenda of church planting in the area entrusted to your care. Ask Him to place thoughts, scriptures, books and people in your life that will help you develop a clear picture of the future within your district. Pray for a clear understanding of His mission for people. After all, He is the One who sent His Son to redeem us back to Himself. If we need clarification of vision and mission, it is certainly appropriate to go back to the One who has the greatest investment in the first place.

2. Intentionally expose yourself to resources that clearly have a church planting focus. Read books such as Bob Logan's, *Beyond Church Growth, How To Implement a Regional Church Planting Vision* and *Church Planter's Toolkit* (co-authored with Steve Ogne); Carl George's, *Prepare Your Church for the Future* and a myriad of other written resources available to you through your own denominational organization and other information that you may know. Spend time with individuals whose lives are driven by the mission of church planting. Identify and meet with successful church planters nearby. Talk to them about their vision, their struggles, their joys and their initial motivation in beginning a new work. Talk with other district leaders who have committed themselves to the church planting agenda. It may be other district overseers. It may be your church leaders, it may be consultants or other individuals whom you know to be directly involved in church planting. Let their vision soak into the fiber of your thinking. Don't try to analyze what they have done, simply listen for the principles and motivation informing what they are doing. No two church planters are the same and no two district movements will be the same. You are not looking for a program to implement; you are looking for energy that causes movement.

3. Talk to those within your own district who are lay or clergy leaders. Listen to what they say and to the spirit in their speaking. By their words they will communicate to you the need for creating a regional church planting movement. They will do so either by direct affirmation or by demonstrating such a void of interest that you will see quickly they have been drained of their mission energy through long years of focusing on the established institution. Your intent is neither to debate nor to convince but simply to listen and let the

Holy Spirit be at work within you through what you hear and see.

4. At some point after much prayer, investigation, openness, resourcing and general input from many sources, you will come to a point where you must make an intentional and willful decision regarding the role of church planting in your life, in your ministry and in your district. This is the appropriate time to make that decision. Without it any effort to plant a church will be sabotaged. You as the leader of your organization must be clear and decisive about the priority of church planting. Others must hear your commitment and know that it is not simply a desire or another one of many secondary programs. They must hear it as a priority commitment that is integral to your total vision and mission.

5. Pray more about what you have seen and heard. Now ask God to give you one or two individuals on whom you can rely for strategic guidance and advice in establishing a church planting movement. They may be consultants with parachurch organizations, other denominational leaders or a district overseer. In any case don't make the mistake of assuming that you will be able to do it by yourself. It's absolutely essential that you glean insight and understanding from others who can not only provide objective points of view but who may have been through the same process before you. Learn from their mistakes, listen carefully to their suggestions. Allow them to be involved for an extended period of time as you begin to move your district into a new priority.

6. Count the cost. Creating a church planting movement will require all you can bring to it. You will need trained facilitators for your components. You'll

need one coach for each church planter and one for each parent church. You'll need key lay leaders to be fully committed with you. Obstacles to new paradigms will need to be removed — opinions, structures and people. You will need money for training in each component and for supplemental support of new churches.

7. Consider your span of control. You may be fully engrossed in your new church planting system when a call comes regarding a crisis requiring your full attention and presence. Will the system then be put on hold while you divert your attention? Don't expect it to build momentum that way. You will probably come to a point where you need to hand it to someone else for oversight. It may be a director of church planting, who is paid. This is ideal because it provides consistent oversight by a high caliber, experienced leader. He or she needs to understand the system well. Such a person must have experience as a planter and have a mind for systems. He or she will be your right arm in mission so choose well. Don't be afraid to take this step. You are not losing control. You are simply freeing yourself to keep casting the vision and comprehensively guide the district in its mission. Further, you are allowing an expert who is focused exclusively on its success to give the system the ongoing attention it warrants.

Overseer, you must prayerfully and thoughtfully assist your pastors and lay leaders in coming to full ownership of mission-driven, ministry-minded action toward a church planting movement. You will need to become different things to different people in order to bring them along with your newfound vision. That's not to say you will be wishy-washy or indecisive. You will just recognize the need to relate differently to people in effecting your goals. In some cases you must:

1. *Cheer them on.* It may be the easiest role to assume. Support those who are pressing ahead with prayerful energy and finding good results. They may not be doing it the way you might, but recognize the positive principles and affirm their vision and action.

2. *Get out of their way.* Ego may suffer when the realization suddenly hits that they do not need your expertise in order to function. They may know more and have more experience. It may simply be that they have it all together. For you to assume that they need help may be a misplaced if not crippling assumption. Your greatest ministry may be to affirm them and stay out of the way. They are bright enough to call if they need help. Even at that, allow them the freedom to call someone else as a resource instead of you. Such trust is the foundation of a good relationship that will incline them to turn to you when your help is needed.

3. *Resource them.* You may have access to tapes, videos, books, speakers and other resources that your people may not. While you may not be able to teach some of your people a great deal, you can keep a constant flow of positive, relevant information moving their direction. Your heart for your leaders will unleash many creative ways to expose them to good input that is consistent with your philosophy of ministry and vision for the district church planting movement.

4. *Channel them.* These people may have all the vision and energy to last a lifetime but may struggle with how to apply it. Often in such a case secondary attachments will develop that sap their energy and diffuse their ministry. The result is frustration, antagonism and eventually burnout. Come alongside these folks and begin to help them build the banks to channel the flood into a river of ministry power. Be careful

not to presume that you need to provide energy. They'll supply that; you guide in channeling it. Give them the help needed and be ready to step back.

5. *Restrain them.* In some respects this is a good problem to have. It sure is better than having to motivate. Yet there are times when unbridled enthusiasm or misguided strategies can lead to conflict within the church, district, or denomination. Quiet and gentle restraint may be called upon to prevent a problem. Two very important principles in restraining such aggressiveness are: 1) Never operate in a high-handed, autocratic, dictatorial style. Other leaders are watching to see if you inherently believe in them or are trying to accomplish some other agenda. 2) Do everything in your power to keep a positive relationship with these people. Remember, connectionalism is primarily relational, and you will be working with these leaders in the future. If they believe you have dealt honestly and with integrity, your ministry to them will continue. Further, such trying experiences can serve as the best opportunities for modeling the personal identity that fuels your ministry.

6. *Protect them.* This may be the most difficult to discuss, much less fulfill, because sometimes it is the denomination or hierarchy from which you must protect leaders. There will be times when something will attempt to encroach on or pressure your key people. In many cases it is appropriate; in others it is not. Your default response should be to stand between your people and the source unless it is obvious such pressure is appropriate. This is particularly true in the case of your church planters. Inherently they are sodalic. In other words, they are action-oriented doers who epitomize movement. Sometimes district and denominational modalities or bureaucratic institutions don't under-

stand this type of person. Their tendency is to discount them and pressure them to conform. Protect your people and interpret each to the other.

7. *Pastor them.* At strategic decision points in life even pastors, planters and lay leaders are insecure, discouraged and alone. Recognize the signs and become a pastor to them. This role probably needs the least amount of discussion because it is the heart of the overseer's calling. To rejoice when they rejoice, to weep when they weep, to pray, love, confront, listen and affirm — that, too, is your role. Simply be the pastor you are and were called to be.

CHAPTER 3 –
PHILOSOPHY

Phases of Becoming

After you have made the commitment to lead your district in becoming a church planting movement but before you actually begin constructing your system, a few issues bear careful attention and thought.

Historically the beginning of new churches has been tied to the catalytic nature of traveling evangelists. The old Methodist circuit riders were given a specific geographic area, and they would cluster groups of people in the small rural towns of America. Largely the success of traveling evangelists was due to their personality and their ability to organize a band of people that subsequently would become a local church. A classic example is the great-grandfather of one of my close friends who, in the course of his life, began 53 churches in the Ohio Valley.

Over the past few decades, we have generally seen a shift in the nature of ministry and leadership. It is increasingly less tied to individual personality and more to shared ministry. The great prophetic leaders of a generation ago are not being replaced with like people. Rather the new cadre of leaders that is rising is characterized as "strategic mobilizers." Someone asked, "Who will replace Billy Graham?" The answer from a rising evangelical leader was, "a team." Mission-driven, pragmatic, ministry-minded, networking teams are increasingly the pattern within the church.

With this shift the institutional church has become less and less focused. Without the prophetic leader driving the institution by force of personality, movement has slowed and the first phase of a major paradigm shift within the church has presented itself.

This first phase is *stagnation*. The stagnation of many church districts has frustrated pastors and lay leaders alike. They rack their brains trying to figure out "Why can't we grow?" In this phase, success in the church has been redefined to mean full file cabinets, monthly reports, the number of active pastors with a seminary education, 100 percent participation in financial allocations and a generally well-greased institutional machine. Comfortable institutionalism puts priority on maintaining the status quo. Purity of our ranks and faithfulness to our past is more important than mission. The statistical reports of new converts and new members may be declining or at best reaching a plateau. However, committee structure and management systems are so well defined and developed that people are lulled into a false sense of security.

The corporate mind and attitude of the district becomes dull and diffused instead of sharp and focused on mission. So instead of being like a sharp-hulled speed boat knifing its way through the water with momentum toward a goal, we gradually but inexorably wind up as a flat-fronted barge, dead in the water due to drag and resistance. In a vain attempt to restart the engines and get going again, we call for more committee work to decide on goals and strategy. The intent is good, yet in this case we find ourselves in a vicious cycle — generating paperwork and committees to help us get beyond merely generating paperwork and committees. This is modality at its worst. This stagnation is a death trap.

Yet within the context of this phase, God can begin to shape the nature of a movement. Increasingly, dissatisfaction with the district gives rise to energy that eventually must be channeled. Once sufficient dissatisfaction with the stagnant phase builds, transition to phase two will begin. The role of leadership is critical at this point in order to begin focusing the energy into productive action. Failure of leadership here will almost certainly result in a total breakdown, division, explosion or mass exodus of catalytic movers.

Howard Snyder reports that the division of the Pentecostal movement from the holiness groups in the early 20th century had little to do with theology and a lot to do with personality. The Pentecostal bands were filled with aggressive, catalytic, sodalic people. This personality dynamic created such tension within the holiness groups that a parting occurred. In most cases this type of exodus not only strips the main body of its progressive energy but leaves those departing with little stability.

A few years ago a good friend of mine grew frustrated with the cumbersome bureaucracy and lack of vision in his denomination. He had planted a church and led it in explosive growth. He is a highly catalytic person who chafed under the restraints of an institution. Finally, he surrendered his ordination credentials and "went independent." Today he's back "home" and is one of the district's strongest advocates for connectionalism. I must hasten to say that his denomination experienced significant refocusing and renewal in mission. This coupled with his own growth and maturity has made for a healthful understanding and balance.

The same principle is illustrated in the sad story of a district I watched over 13 years. I was not personally involved in it but was able to see general patterns emerging. It wasn't large but it was highly organized and institutionalized. Leadership was virtually nonexistent. Success was tacitly understood to be full compliance with all procedures and no boat rocking. Any time an energetic, catalytic pastor would begin to show signs of breaking into significant growth it was squelched. The leader had little tolerance for the creative diversity represented by these progressive people. One after another they left for more tolerant and progressive environments. The district became a study in sameness. The churches looked the same and the pastors looked the same. Everything was flat. It was as if the point were removed from the arrow. No one was left to stretch the group in innovation, growth or challenge. Without those marines leading the charge, the district began to think its mission was simply to resupply itself and stay exactly the way it was. All of the catalytic movers had left because leadership had failed to recognize their value and channel their energy into productive movement toward Kingdom mission.

Phase two is characterized as the *shotgun* phase. It is almost the opposite of the stagnant phase. In this phase all energies are focused upon immediate deployment of any individual wishing to start a new church. All financial resources and time are spent on the front lines. Sometimes movement from phase one to phase two is extremely painful and divisive because the pendulum has swung to the other extreme. Individuals who have been frustrated in the stagnant mode have created such dissatisfaction that now people within the district are at odds with one another. The new emphasis on church planting may even have a tendency to breed discontent in and of itself. Inasmuch as it represents the antithesis of the status quo, it becomes the culprit for disturbing the peace. Those once comfortable with the status quo and antagonistic to the change agents, may allow their skepticism of a new emphasis to develop into division, based on the fact of change and not because of the new focus on church planting. The shotgun phase is not necessarily enjoyable. Nevertheless, movement has begun. The gun is discharging and something will happen. Unfortunately there is little direction, consistency, coherence and focus to the energy. Virtually any individual who expresses a need or desire to become a church planter is immediately deployed with little or no training or support. Funds are allocated based more on the urgency of the need than on thoughtful preplanning. While the shotgun phase results in church planting activity it does not build long term stability and health. Just as invading marines must have supply ships and replacement systems to allow for continued progress, so also the energy for church planting requires systems that will continue to fuel it and develop its health. It's at this point that phase three must engage.

Timing in encouraging movement to phase three is critical. Premature efforts will meet with resistance and accusations of a return to bureaucracy. The sodalic or action-minded people have not yet realized that all water and no banks make for a flood. Patience, leader. They'll come to it. Conversely, too much delay in leaving the shotgun phase can allow internal strife and antagonism to go so deep that it becomes counterproductive and even irreparable. Here is where your conscientious attention to personal preparation early on will really pay off. You will know the timing as you infuse your vision, which you have carefully nurtured, into your people, whom you have carefully cultivated.

A church planting *system* provides for focus, targeting, health and direction. In effect the system becomes the "banks" that direct the energy flow of the river. Instead of a flood we must channel the new church planting energy into productive results.

In 1985 as I traveled to central Africa with my overseer, Clyde Van Valin, he told me a story of one of his previous visits to Zaire. During a particularly dry year near one of our hospitals the river in the mountain above the hospital had dried up. Not expecting such an occurrence, the missionaries and nationals had requested from the United States the last piece of a hydroelectric generator they were installing at the river to provide energy for the hospital compound. The following year the rains came and the river was filled to overflowing. The water gushed down the mountain with unusual power. As Reverend Van Valin and one of the nationals watched the flow, amazed at the raw energy it represented, they grew concerned over the potential damage the raging water might cause.

As we reflected together on his memory, the irony was apparent. That which the people needed to fulfill their mission had come, but with such unbridled fury that it now posed a possible danger. The difference between destructive and constructive power? The final piece of the generator that would activate the systems to channel the power of the river in fulfilling the mission.

The transition to a new system may be as difficult as the transition from stagnation to shotgun. The commitment to develop a church planting system requires pulling resources from frontline activities and reappropriating them to support networks and delivery systems. This process can be extremely difficult for the aggressive, sodality-minded leader. It may require a hiatus of actual church planting while the system is constructed, much like a river may need to be diverted while generator systems are installed.

At the same time the leader must be capable of understanding that emphasis must now be placed on the delivery systems if new births are going to be healthy and successful. There is a danger at this point of being accused of once again "building the institution." Presumably the district constituency has seen the mission-minded vision of the leader, and they will trust him or her not to return to the old institutional approach. The relationships of trust built in vision casting and leading the district to this point must now be relied upon for continued unity in becoming a system. At every point mission must remain paramount. If people are able to see how the building of a structure relates to the fulfillment of mission they will follow leadership.

Although the office of district overseer has come to be an institution in most denominations, it does not need to assume the characteristics of impotence and inflexibility, which often accompany institutionalization. Overseers will mean the difference between success and failure in becoming a church planting movement. For you to be successful in that role, you must understand the careful balance between movement and institution.

Many times the aggressive young doers wish they could just dump the institution. Conversely the institution types feel as though they are always being attacked by the rebellious, young upstarts. In fact, we need both.

The healthy church is one continuum represented at the ends by institution and movement; modality and sodality; bureaucrats and entrepreneurs (Figure 2).

Institution		Movement
Modality	Healthy Church Balance	Sodality
Bureaucrats	■	Entrepreneurs

Figure 2

Eliminate one side of the continuum and the church gets out of balance. Institution without movement is *stagnation*. Movement without institution is *shotgun*. Both in balance provide a creative and effective *system* which epitomizes health.

Sodality and modality are terms described by Ralph Winter in 1973 at the All-Asian Mission Consultation in Korea. They represent God's two redemptive structures. Sam Metcalf, President of CRM has further focused the concepts. Generally, modalities are the church in parish or local church form. Sodalities are the church in highly focused, task-oriented agencies to which we have traditionally given the misnomer, "parachurch organization." They are not separate from the church. They are the church. Characteristics of each should exist in the healthy, growing church. Sodality and modality are two sides of the same coin. Each is necessary for wholeness. Each has its role in fulfilling the mission. To think that either can operate without the other is a serious mistake that only leads to death on the one hand or chaos on the other. Christian leaders must find a careful balance between our human instinct for order and our impulse for chaos.

Bureaucrats without entrepreneurs will wind up in a vicious cycle of self-preservation and protectionism. Entrepreneurs without bureaucrats will find themselves with shallow, disorganized, flash-in-the-pan programs. We really are one body with many parts. Under a common mission and with focused energy the body can be healthy and balanced. This is effective movement.

Core Values of a System

There are a few core values that must be inherent and uncompromising in any church planting system. The first of these is a focus on *production capacity*. Covey describes the difference between emphasizing production capacity versus product. A focus on production capacity brings energies to bear on building systems and factories for production not on individual cases. In other words, instead of planting one church at a time, production capacity will focus on building the systems and the factories that will produce multiple churches.

Covey illustrates his principle with the fable of "The Goose that Laid the Golden Egg." The poor farmer grew so excited about waking up each morning to a golden egg that he became obsessed with the wealth it represented. In his greed he purposed to kill the goose and get all the golden eggs at once instead of waiting for one each day. His impatience for the golden egg and wealth — product, caused him to destroy the goose that was the source — production capacity.

Consider the more contemporary example of modern airlines. With deregulation came intense competition merely for survival. Some went to great measures to increasing profits to maintain viability and growth — product. In so doing they removed a few extras in service, pushed their employees through reduced benefits and worked their equipment harder with minimum maintenance. While short-term results appeared good, gradually such an intense fixation on product caught up with them. Their equipment, employees and relationship to passengers — production capacity, had been neglected. The goose was sick and dying. Employees began to complain, which impacted their work and attitude with the public. Equipment began to fail. Passengers noticed the reduction in service. A serious crash due to equipment fatigue, an employee strike with national attention, a significant inconvenience to passengers were merely symptoms of an operational paradigm focused exclusively on product.

Years ago my uncle owned a restaurant in Jackson, Michigan. Mannoia's Spaghetti House was a popular place, especially for the college community in nearby Spring Arbor. The atmosphere was great, the food exceptional and the singing chef — Uncle Joe himself — always showed interest in his customers and work. Business was good and Mannoia's had a reputation. At his retirement Uncle Joe sold the business. Part of the agreement was that the name would go with it. The buyer knew of the reputation and wanted to capitalize on the name. At first he succeeded. However, he was too interested in the profits of the business to invest in that which had caused it to be profitable. The atmosphere deteriorated, the food was only passable and the customers didn't feel special. Soon there were no more crowds after the basketball game. It wasn't the place to go. People stopped talking about it and the reputation was lost. The new owner failed to understand production capacity. He didn't invest in the source of the product. He neglected the careful balance between results and the ability to produce.

You can probably think of many of your own examples. Suffice it to say that although attention to product in the district is important — planting churches, a careful balance must be maintained. The production capacity of the district must be carefully developed and nurtured for long-term success. If church planting is the product of the district, then mission and philosophy of church planting, a comprehensive and integrated system and relationships with churches and key growth leaders all represent production capacity. The traditional church district tends to operate by focusing on single addition to its numbers. Perhaps it's because there is such little movement that we grow excited about one new church after years of existence. The addition of single churches over the course of many years will not result in the kind of growth of which the church is capable. District overseers may even tend to bring their personal influence and involvement to bear on one church plant at a time. If that one church plant is successful everyone feels good for the time being, but the whole process must begin over when another plant is begun. Often so much energy has been expended on that one single plant that leadership is weary and feels it must take a break before involving itself in such a high level of energy commitment. In the process leaders change, district overseers are replaced, budgets are altered and focus is lost.

To emphasize production capacity means that energies will be expended in the building of "factories" that are interrelated and self-perpetuating in the production of new churches. It's not so cold and impersonal as it sounds because a multiplicity of people are involved in the process. If we can successfully instill the concept of production capacity within our districts, we can guarantee its success and reproduction for years if not decades to come. We are, in effect, streamlining the ability to plant churches. They are then planted not singly but plurally.

A second core value is the concept of *franchising*. This concept goes as far back as the Exodus when Jethro prompted Moses to franchise himself in others for increased effectiveness. More recently the secular world has been reminded of the importance of franchising in Michael Gerber's book, *The E Myth*. As Gerber points out, franchising a prototype "... is the medium through which [the entrepreneur's] vision takes form in the real world." Bob Logan and his colleagues at Church Resource Ministries have been developing this concept in church application in what they call "reproducible systems." It's a multiyear effort that will be described exhaustively in future writings.

Within the total church planting movement, Logan asserts that systems must be developed that can easily be replicated at another time or location. He points to the experience and results of revivalists George Whitefield and John Wesley. Both were equally powerful in their preaching and influence in their own day. Both saw untold numbers come to personal saving faith in Jesus Christ. Yet a significant difference exists between the two. Today the entire Wesleyan movement has its roots in the work of John Wesley. We read about George Whitefield in the history books. The difference? Wesley's emphasis was on "societies" or cell groups and structural systems that could duplicate themselves in another time or in another place.

Such an emphasis provided a systematic channel for the revival energy of the 18th century to become the Methodist movement. Subsequently it crossed the Atlantic and spawned the Methodist Episcopal Church and many other denominations that have major influence in the world to this day.

If we look at denominations from a macro point of view, we realize that many of the connectional systems contain the franchising concept within themselves. There is connection in organization, finance, procedures and theology. With a certain degree of centralization many of the basics of church life are simply replicated in various local settings. In this heritage and tradition, the basic emotional understanding and commitment exists in which franchising can be understood and applied with great success. The basic paradigm is, therefore, already extant and the ability to understand it is greater. It makes the paradigm shift to becoming a church planting movement far smoother and more easily accepted.

Thirdly, any effort in becoming a church planting movement must be characterized as being *pragmatic*. Energies expended, time spent, money invested, must have a clear result in fulfilling the goal of planting churches and thus growing the Kingdom. If it doesn't work, don't do it. If by previous experience positive results can be verified, time and energy must be invested to make it work. Obviously that means that district leaders must be aware of what is working in other places. That gives rise to a fourth core value of a system.

A *shared attitude* must be prevalent in all activities in becoming a church planting system. That means that interdenominational communication and cooperation links must be built. Fences between the church and parachurch organizations must be removed. There is no reason to reinvent the wheel. There are many places where successful church planting is happening. Lessons learned can easily be shared. Within the context of the contemporary church the spirit of cooperation and shared ministry is being continuously fueled by heightened commitment to mission and growth. Increasingly, leaders are pragmatic in nature and committed to do whatever is necessary to lead their constituents in expanding their influence for Christ.

Very few individual districts will have the ability to build an entire church planting system on their own. Cooperation will be absolutely essential with like-minded denominations and parachurch organizations.

Strategic Shift

Districts do not beget churches, churches do. If there is one phrase that characterizes the strategic shift to becoming a church planting movement, this is it. Too often our districts attempt to become parents when in reality it shouldn't be their responsibility. It's sort of like grandparents trying to have children. That's not their job; that's the parents' job. Grandparents, as districts, exist to provide a nurturing healthful environment in which a healthy birth can take place.

One of the most difficult adjustments of the district overseer will be continually to remind himself that the onus of responsibility for church planting must be with the local church. His or her task must be to provide the environment in which those local churches can become "pregnant" and ultimately "parents." This transition, however, is absolutely essential if the core value of production capacity is to become reality. Every document, every position paper, every speech, every report should remind the district that the responsibility for church planting is upon the local church not the district.

The district must be ready to provide the care necessary for the local churches to reproduce. Parent churches need prenatal and midwife care. The district must be willing to invest itself in providing the preparation systems for a parent church to give birth to a healthy, thriving and successful new church.

Districts contain within themselves the seeds of their own reproduction — the local churches. Failure to invest in the development and nurturing of these seeds will naturally result in the return to a stagnant phase where growth has leveled off or is declining. Conversely, careful, intentional and consistent nurturing of those seeds will result in local churches becoming refocused, pregnant and eventually giving birth to healthy offspring. That's the goal of the church planting system.

Critical Points in Parenting

It will be helpful for the overseer to understand a few critical points in the process of parenting a church. It will be of great value in assisting the local church to become a parent congregation. Once the weight of responsibility for planting churches is clearly upon the local church, the district and its leadership must demonstrate an understanding and commitment to assist that church through these various critical points.

1. Conception is owned by the body. At some point the seed of church planting must be placed within the heart and mind of a local congregation. Church planting, like human birth, requires total-body involvement. It may require a period of time for the concept and vision of becoming a parent church to soak into a majority of the church constituency. It's at this point that the district system can assist a local pastor and key

lay leaders in vision casting and removing potential obstacles to becoming healthy parents.

2. The church planter is identified. There can be no new church without a church planter. In many respects the planter becomes the embodiment of the seed embedded within the local church body. Planter identification is perhaps the most underrated factor in beginning a new church. Too many individuals have been discouraged, disillusioned, or otherwise broken in a failed attempt to begin a new church. The identification of an effective church planter requires careful scrutiny and effective systems that will result in a qualified church planter.

3. Gestation within the parent. The idea of planting a new church does not move to reality within a short period of time. Opportunity for the planter to gain familiarity with the parent and identify core families requires time. A minimum of three months is necessary for this process to occur. Ideally six months would be allowed for the parent church to come to full term. Obviously much is dependent on the level of readiness of the congregation when the concept is first considered. The number of obstacles that must be removed is also a significant factor in the length of gestation.

4. Birth is clear and decisive. Some of the most difficult efforts of church planting have been characterized by a gradual trickling of people from the parent to the new church. The birth of a new church should be quick and decisive and celebrated by everyone. Plans should be laid for the birth day to occur. It should be clear in the minds of the planter, core families, parent congregation and community that a new church has begun. Failure to do so may result in a gradual bleeding to death of either the parent or the new church.

5. Postpartum is anticipated. To think that a parent congregation can give away significant core families and a high profile catalytic church planter without suffering is a myth. I recall the Sunday after a grand celebration in which we commissioned 25 core people and the church planter to go and begin a new church. That Sunday was perhaps the most discouraging and somber day of the year. My staff pastor was not beside me, many key people were not present in the congregation before me and part of my heart was in another place. To understand and acknowledge the reality of postpartum blues is an essential ingredient in understanding the total birth process. Anticipate and plan for it.

6. Neo-natal care is ready and effective. No new church will be able to survive without immediate and careful support to nurture it through the early days of its existence. We don't expect a new church to have the level of leadership maturity, financial stability, ministry breadth or community involvement as an established church of 50 years. Systems capable of nurturing a new church through its early days must be developed and ready to be activated immediately upon the day of birth. These systems should carry a new church through its first two years of life and, if necessary, longer until maturity is evident within the new church.

CHAPTER 4 –
SYSTEM

A Reminder

Let's turn our attention now to the specifics of the Century 21 System. While this may appear to be the most important part of becoming a church planting movement, we cannot underestimate the importance of the first three chapters. It may be tempting to begin your investigation at this point and skip the "deeper stuff" and more "tedious" conceptual portions. To do so would be a mistake and fatal to the end result. It would relegate the entire concept of church planting to nothing more than another prepackaged program to be bought, imported and superimposed. Nothing could be further from the truth.

Go back and read the first three chapters. They represent the triad of support footers on which the entire superstructure rests — Mission, Leadership, Philosophy. Omitting them, or any one of them, is like building a house on the sand.

Don't assume your recently discovered curiosity for church planting will provide sufficient support for the commitment required of you. Don't think you can do a cursory once over on the big points and assign it to your evangelism committee for implementation. Let me remind you, we're talking about a movement, an attitude, a sodality. If nothing else, appease me by giving careful attention to chapters 1-3. Perhaps only to validate my time and energy in writing them, but most of all for the possibility that God may do something in you through them.

An Overview

The Century 21 Church Planting System is an umbrella system comprised of ten components. Each component is 1) free-standing, 2) modular and 3) reproducible. That is, each of the ten components is neither connected to nor dependent upon any of the others. They can be fully operational independently. However, for maximum effectiveness they must complement each other. While there is no particular sequencing required for implementation, there is a somewhat natural progression, which will become clear. Further, each component is intentionally designed to be plugged in at the time and place it is needed in the overall system development. Each can be franchised across district and denominational lines. As well, some of the components may require more than one application in the same district to accommodate the demand at a particular time. The components have been conceived, developed and implemented by different experts as noted in the following list and in Appendix B. In this way your district can benefit from the best work done in each of the many areas required for a church planting movement.

While each component is significant in the total system, don't assume that all of them can be up and running quickly. It may require up to five years to make the entire system fully operational. In light of this, pick the first two or three components carefully. Although circumstances unique to your district may require implementing one before another, the first three listed are top priority and are considered core to the entire system.

CENTURY 21
CHURCH PLANTING SYSTEM

A comprehensive and cohesive strategy for developing a regional church planting movement.

1. *Parent Church Network.* Enables pastors and key leaders to cultivate congregational commitment to church planting and design/implement an effective strategy resulting in a new congregation within two years. (Logan and Ogne)

2. *Profile Assessment System.* Establishes objective and intensive processes for assessing skills, performance and personality profile in prospective planters.

3. *New Church Incubator.* Provides a supportive environment, skill training and coaching relationships for planters, their spouses and key lay leaders from conception through the first year after public worship begins. (Logan and Ogne)

4. *Recruitment Network.* Establishes an intentional strategy for recruiting a pool of pastoral candidates particularly focusing on those with church planting interest and proficiency.

5. *Pastor Factory.* Trains proven lay leaders to become founding pastors and lifelong learners through internship, mentoring and biblical study with small group interaction. (Cole and Logan)

6. *Church Planters' Summit.* A retreat designed to orient church planters with the Century 21 Church

Planting System and its motivating philosophy within the district or regional context. (Moore)

7. *Maturing Church Cluster.* Assists new churches in the first five years to identify and navigate the major paradigm shifts required in maturing into a healthy and growing church.

8. *Strategic Planning Network.* Networks pastors and lay leaders in diagnosing and planning to lead their churches in breaking growth barriers and developing a commitment to start a new church.

9. *Harvest 1000.* Provides opportunity for focused emphasis on church plants through developing a supplemental financial network of regional lay leaders.

10. *Meta-Church Network.* Clusters pastors of churches committed to understanding and implementing meta-church principles through equipping, study and diagnosis according to a prescribed curriculum. (Fitch)

It may be a little intimidating to read this list with the description of each component and realize the time, energy and work it requires for implementation. Don't be afraid. It's not so overwhelming as it seems. Each of the components has already been conceived, developed, pilot tested and reproduced. You need not reinvent the wheel. The experts behind each one are fully at your disposal through their writing and training.

Don't expect to have a working knowledge of each component, much less of their interactive relationships, before you begin. Your knowledge of and commitment to the total system will flow from one of two sources.

1. You will become personally aware and involved in one of the components to such a degree that an emotional connection and enthusiasm for church planting will result. Out of that enthusiasm will come the energy to deal with other issues or problems that will naturally arise in the church planting enterprise. You will be motivated by your interest and commitment to solve the problems facing you. That will naturally lead you to each of the other components as an answer to your situation.

For example, let's say that after you commit to explore church planting in your area, you attend a training session for the Parent Church Network (PCN). As a result you identify five churches in your area who commit to a PCN. After three or four months of training you begin to realize that church planters must be identified. That leads you to expand your Recruitment Network. After developing a pool of candidates, you learn firsthand that not all candidates are equal. Each is gifted differently and "wired" uniquely. How do you know which ones will be successful? There are great differences between pastoring an existing church and planting a new church. Your investigation in developing a philosophy (chapter 3) and mission awareness (chapter 1) yielded that knowledge. What criteria do you use to discriminate between gifts and behavior required of a planter compared to those of a pastor? Never fear, the Profile Assessment System (PAS) exists for that purpose.

Knowing also that there are circumstances and trials unique to getting a new church started, you provide a warm, supportive environment in which your planters can develop. It's the New Church Incubator (NCI). To establish relational bonding and personal rapport, you plan a Church Planters' Summit (CPS).

Understanding that as the planters are assessed in the PAS and nurtured in the NCI and as the PCN produces "pregnant" churches you must also begin to assist the "baby" with finances and support for problems encountered by the "newborn." So you inquire and discover the Harvest 1000 plan that will supplement the local church budget and the Maturing Church Cluster (MCC) designed for the first five years of life.

All of this is to say, don't be afraid of the magnitude of the total system. Allow the single contact point to develop your involvement and then let your questions lead you naturally into the rest of the system as needed.

2. A second and less likely source of commitment to the total system may come through capturing the energy and spirit of the "macro" view. Perhaps as you contemplate your mission, leadership and philosophy relative to church planting you will begin to comprehend the intricacies and relationships of the ten components in a holistic way. In clarity of operation you may find enthusiastic commitment. Seeing how each component can meet a critical need, work toward a common goal of new churches and develop a commensurate relational bonding in each of the component groups, you will find motivation for action and perseverance.

Whatever the source of commitment and involvement in the Century 21 System, at some point, sooner or later, a comprehensive awareness of the system must develop. Without it each component may fragment and become counterproductive. The key is a common, unifying mission — to make God known through church planting. This unity will allow for cohesive cooperation of all components in the development of a synergistic system of church planting.

Look carefully at the diagram that follows (Figure 3). It takes the ten components and integrates them into a total system. Notice particularly that all of it begins with and flows from prayer. Remember, leader, this is where it all starts in you too (see chapter 2). The Century 21 System operates within the larger context of the district. It is not a tack on. It's not an imported program. It is designed to use the leadership, churches, resources and context of your individual region. It is complementary to any licensure or ordination process your group uses. Within the center triangle you see the three key players identified. Each is positioned to indicate its primary focus of preparation and involvement. The district will be the primary instigator of movement toward church planting thinking. It will nurture vision in its earliest stages in parent churches and planters. In the case of each parent church and planter, a point will come where the district overseer and pastor must make an intentional decision to invest in the church and planter. To do so means they will insert both into the system — the parent church in the track on the right and the planter on the left.

Further, notice the dotted lines in the middle of the "Y." Although Parent Church development and Planter development are on separate tracks, which converge in the new church, a great deal of interaction may occur early in each developmental process. Coupling a planter with a parent may occur at any point along the way. In some cases the parent church has within it the planter candidate from the very start. In other cases the parent and planter are in preparation, and a match doesn't occur until both are well along in the process. Given this high degree of flexibility and dynamic nature, a comprehensive understanding of the total system is all the more important.

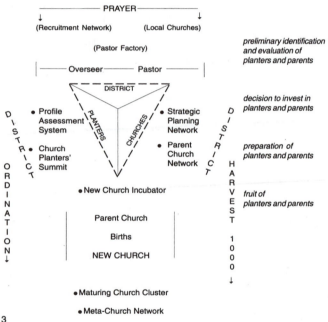

Century 21
Church Planting System

Figure 3

CHAPTER 5 –
COMPONENTS

When my family moved to Brazil as missionaries in 1962, I remember that we took a few things with us that my parents hoped would help to keep the feeling of home. One of the items we shipped was our dark-wood Zenith stereo. It was a large piece of furniture that was given a prominent place in our home. It was not easily moved as stereos go.

Upon our return in 1970 I discovered that the new thing in stereos was not the console, furniture type but rather the integrated component systems. These systems allowed you to start small and build. You had the freedom to mix name brands, select the components desired and position them virtually anywhere in the room. They were modular, mobile, yet capable of being integrated with other components to make a total system.

Similarly the Century 21 System is comprised of component parts. Each is freestanding yet most effective when used in an integrated system. Each has been developed independently by a qualified expert who has your interests at heart. Let's take the time to examine the ten components. As we do, notice the key persons involved in making them successful. There are three.

1. As I mentioned in chapter 2, perhaps the most important person in making your system successful will be a full-time or part-time *director* dedicated to church planting. In effect this is an assistant to the dis-

trict overseer. Make no mistake, this is not someone you hire simply to do the busy work. Nor is it a hired gun to do church planting. This person must be overseer caliber. He or she is a direct and high profile extension of the overseer's ministry. Primary power in mission must still come from the overseer. That power, however, finds embodiment and focus through the regular and consistent attention of the director. One district may not have the ability to support such a position even on a part-time basis. There may be neighboring districts who can partner together for such a position in order to get the ball rolling. This person will need to command the respect of all district leaders and especially those involved in the church planting enterprise. As such, he or she must have a direct connection with successful church planting — preferably as a planter. The director is the expert who will guide the district in fulfilling the overseer's vision of becoming a church planting movement.

If you are an overseer, don't wait until this person is on line before moving into church planting. For a time it may be that this role must rest with you. As movement builds, so will the load. Adding this position will be a natural step and require little convincing in the committees. This is actually the most effective way to get going since it forces a natural integration of the church planting priority into your total ministry.

2. The *facilitator* is the primary resource agent who not only has a general understanding of the entire system, but in effect, is the leader in his or her particular component. This expertise comes, however, not just from a comprehensive knowledge of the material, but also from some degree of personal experience. The facilitator will be the guide/leader of the participants and coaches within the individual component. Because

of this, care should be taken in the selection of the facilitator. He or she must have a good understanding of coaching techniques, as well as the capacity to teach and lead the regular group sessions.

3. If the facilitator is the resource agent, the *coach* is the workhorse. The coach meets individually once a month between regular group sessions with two or three participants. In this way the participant not only has input at the group meeting from the facilitator and other participants, but he or she also has regular, personal coaching individualized for his or her case. While the coach should understand basic coaching techniques, he or she does not need to have the same level of training in the component as the facilitator. The coach's participation in the component will be sufficient to equip him or her. Occasionally, however, the facilitator may take special time with the coaches.

The last two of these key persons (facilitator and coach) are roles that have been developed by Logan and Ogne and are integral to their treatment of reproducible systems. In regular training events they provide general help for these functions and will develop more resources focused on coaching.

As you consider identifying persons within your district who could serve as facilitators and coaches, keep in mind: 1) They should have an emotional connection with church planting. In most cases this means they have actual experience as planters. At least they should have experience as core members of a new church or some other direct involvement with church planting. 2) They should be strategic thinkers. This is especially true of facilitators. They must be able to understand how what they do is motivated by the mission, fits in with the other components and generally impacts the future of the district. 3) They should be sodalic leaders. Simply put, this means they must be action-oriented, proactive doers. There is a place for theorizing. This is not it. You need task-oriented persons who will effectively do the job. Their attitude and track record must demonstrate a higher importance placed on movement toward mission than on discussion.

As you consider the list of components, remember that the top three are core to the system. They are essential if any system is to succeed. Consider again the example of a component stereo system. What are the essentials in making a stereo? Could you get by without an amplifier? No. What about speakers? No. How about a signal source? No. If you have a stereo you have at least these three things. Additionally you may also add multiple signal sources, like a CD player, cassette deck, phonograph, etc. You also may add equalizers, bass boost, surround sound and many other options. All are nice and enhance quality but none work without the basic three.

Similarly, the church planting system requires the first three components. Without any one of these, the system ceases to be a church planting system. To remove these would be tantamount to removing the amplifier, or speakers, or signal source from your stereo. These are essential ingredients without which your stereo is no longer a stereo.

Parent Church Network

*Enables pastors and lay leaders to
cultivate congregational commitment to church planting
and design/implement an effective strategy resulting in a
new congregation within two years.*

I begin with the Parent Church Network (PCN) not only because it is one of the top three components in the Century 21 System but also because it epitomizes the major paradigm shift required within the district. As I mentioned earlier, we must begin to see that the responsibility for church planting rests not with the district (grandparent) but with the local church (parent). The PCN clearly establishes that paradigm. By its existence many signals are sent to the district: 1) Planting churches is a high priority; 2) A coordinated system is the chosen method; 3) Local churches are expected to reproduce themselves; 4) The district will provide the best resourcing possible to help its churches fulfill that goal.

Although it may not be the first in your system, the PCN developed by Logan and Ogne singularly embodies a church planting system more than any other individual component. Further, it does not require a large investment before the district is emotionally ready. It does not require that church planters be fully identified. The PCN captures "pre-planting energy" and channels it through the local church in a coherent constructive way. Even though the PCN requires a basic commitment to parent a church, you're not pushing people to a commitment or a level of expertise. In the PCN you simply recognize the raw church planting interest in a local church and honestly position the district to help that church become what it wants to become — a parent. The district is not a demanding force, but a supporting force; not an institution to be served, but a system to serve. What better way to demonstrate the true relationship between local churches and their umbrella district?

One of the greatest inhibitors for a church to become a parent is the fact that the congregation doesn't know how to do it. In the odd case where a local church plunges ahead into parenting it does so with little or no systematic help. It's almost as though each church making such a commitment has to be the first to learn the path and pitfalls of parenting. No one is there to guide, warn, encourage or reflect. So in effect every parent church is the first one to travel this path. It does so without the coordinated experience of those who have gone before. Often it is only the vision, energy or stamina of the pastor and key lay leaders that powers the parent through the obstacles to success. This relegates the parenting role to a small percentage of churches with exceptionally strong or visionary leaders. In reality it should be a small percentage of churches, those that are especially unhealthy, that would not be able to parent new churches. One thing is true about parenting in any organism: it is integral to completeness and only mitigated by unusual ill health.

The PCN clusters three to five churches for training and mutual support. Each church in the PCN makes a commitment to begin a new congregation within 18-24 months. Every new church plant is unique, yet the principles are similar to all. The PCN is designed to provide training in the principles common to all new church starts while allowing for distinctives. It provides a comprehensive structure to maximize the establishment of new congregations through parent churches.

Now is as good a time as any to make an important point about church planting in the United States. Traditionally we've thought of planting a church in terms of a new and separate church 10 or 15 miles away. Usually the new church is autonomous and independent of sister churches in the district. We must teach ourselves to include new congregations in the term *church planting*. It may be that the best way for a church to reach its community is to start a second or third congregation in the same location. That is just as much church planting as starting a new church in the next town.

With the rise in land and building costs this is more and more attractive. Add to that the increasing need for variety in style of worship as well as the increasing multiethnicity of our communities and you really have a case for planting new congregations in the same location.

There are two legitimate reasons for planting another congregation: 1) alternative worship style and 2) alternative language. It's not my intent to deal comprehensively with multiethnic ministry. I do believe, however, that language is a legitimate reason to start a new congregation. Ethnicity is not. Likewise different worship styles may reach different groups of people without compromising the core values of a church. To expand in this multicongregational way may be the most responsible, community-relevant way to grow.

Please understand, this is not the same as having multiple services due to facility constraints. I'm speaking of intentional efforts to reach different people with the same message and develop a new congregation with its own identity and characteristics.

Churches who make a commitment to starting a new congregation on these terms should view themselves as prospective parents and be included in the PCN. As the PCN grows in experience, the unique needs of these types of parents will be more comprehensively addressed.

A few years ago I made arrangements for Bob Logan to meet with a group of my pastors to discuss meta-church principles. The group had been meeting for about a year, and I simply wanted to resource them. After the meeting over lunch I told Bob of my plan to cluster churches that had the capacity to launch new church plants. I wasn't sure what I would tell them. I just knew that if I could get them together and point them in the direction of church planting, nature would take its course and we would probably have some new bouncing baby churches on our hands.

I asked Bob for advice regarding content. Come to find out, he and Steve Ogne had been working on similar concepts. The result was a marriage made in heaven and the probability of countless new churches in the future. (At some point you're going to wonder how far we can take the analogy of marriage, parent, birth, grandparent, etc. Just wait, it goes further.) Bob and Steve agreed to design a process, and I promised to provide district funds for development, clustering the churches, pilot testing and working with implementation.

With only eight-months experience, the PCN represented a solid commitment to eight new churches within 12-24 months. That should be compared to my goal of two per year in the shotgun stage (see chapter 3). If ever I had doubts about the new paradigms of a church planting system, that fact erased them all.

Once each four to eight weeks the pastor and a team of key leaders from each participating church meet for the network meeting. This is an intensive training and group-building time. The facilitator guides the group through the PCN process as developed by Logan and Ogne. Individuals identified as coaches are also part of these meetings. Coaches may be some of the participating pastors, if the facilitator and overseer determine they are capable.

Between each network meeting, the coaches plan a one-to-one meeting with the pastors assigned to them. During these sessions individual guidance can be given for the particulars of each church. Obviously accountability is a high priority in these meetings as is encouragement and prayer. Approximately every two to four weeks, then, the pastor of the parent church is helped to prepare his or her church to give birth. This is prenatal care at its best.

Generally the process centers around three phases. 1) Preparing for Parenthood, 2) Planning for Parenthood and 3) Proceeding With Parenthood. It helps church leaders identify objections and blockages to being a parent church. It helps identify and deal with key opinion leaders. It assists each prospective parent to develop a sound financial plan for the new church. It cultivates commitment, strategy and resources. It prepares the church for birth and postpartum blues. It helps with recovery, debriefing and evaluation and introduces the availability of the other components at the right time. All of this under the careful watch of a facilitator, a coach and with the support of others in the same process.

I realize that clustering even a small group of churches committed to parenting may be a difficult task. Some districts do not have a general understanding or commitment sufficient to yield such a group. In this case, the PCN may not be the first component to be implemented. You may need to begin with planting a few churches in the shotgun stage (see chapter 3). After some movement has begun and awareness raised, a few pastors may emerge with sufficient interest and commitment to warrant consideration of a PCN. District leaders will need to judge the condition of their district. Be careful not to expect more of your leaders and churches than they are able to deliver. An intense and extended period of education may be necessary before the first components are developed. This is all part of creating the proper environment. Integral to this environment is the support, involvement and commitment of the district pastors. Because pastors are the primary assets of any district, a majority of them must be at least supportive if not involved. Without this, any effort to develop a church planting system will fail. Heavy investment in your pastors to bring them to a common mind in this mission is critical.

So while your first component may not be a PCN, after the environment is established it will be necessary to a true church planting system. The PCN has at its core the assumption that other components are ready and waiting — especially the New Church Incubator and the Profile Assessment System. Although it can begin without the other two being in place, the PCN can only be fully effective in coordination with them at the appropriate time.

Profile Assessment System

*Establishes objective and intensive
processes for assessing skills, performance
and personality profile in prospective planters.*

If the Parent Church Network embodies the primary paradigms of a church planting movement, the Profile Assessment System (PAS) is the component that will have the greatest short-term impact on the district planting efforts. The PAS raises the success rate of new churches by focusing on the most important ingredient — the planter. As I've already said, the church rises and falls on leadership. Given this reality, if we improve our selection of individuals deployed as planters, we also increase the probability that our church planting efforts will be healthy and successful.

There is evidence that effective assessment of church planters is up to 90 percent accurate in the long term. That is, 90 percent of those evaluated and recommended by competent assessors were successful in their church planting effort. With that amazingly high rate of discrimination between qualified and unqualified planters and with the success or failure of church planting efforts riding so heavily upon the leader, can you imagine how much more successful we would be at starting new churches if only we would use a PAS?

One district reports a 34 percent success rate in church planting with no specialized evaluation of planter prospects. Simply implementing an effective PAS could raise that success rate by at least 100 percent. In that same district the failed attempts represented over $550,000, years of time and energy and 11 careers.

That's an investment with no fruit; the proverbial black hole. Imagine what you could do with those resources.

Assessing potential planters and screening out those who are not qualified is more than a numbers game. It is a matter of stewardship. Can we in good conscience invest God's resources — people, money, time — in something with such a low rate of return? If we can improve our decision making with modest up-front costs, shouldn't we?

Implementing the PAS at a relatively small cost in time and money will result in an immediate improvement in church planting ventures. Obviously it means that we must be ready to say "no" to some sincere and well-meaning candidates. In fact, for every candidate recommended for deployment, three to five could be redirected to ministries other than church planting. So you see why the PAS will have the most immediate impact on the district church planting enterprise. There is a 90 percent chance that the first candidate recommended for deployment by the PAS will succeed. Every one thereafter will be similarly successful. Movement, energy and momentum is the synergistic result in the district.

A comprehensive PAS is built upon a triad of evaluations, the third of which is the focus of this component in the Century 21 System. Those three parts are: Personality, Performance, Skills.

I assume that most districts have some plan already in place for assessing the personality profile of ministerial candidates. Usually this is done by a professional counselor or counseling center in the district. Some use the MMPI; others, the Myers-Briggs. Whatever instrument is used, it is important to provide some type of screening for personality. Screening is generally a common practice so I'll not spend time discussing it.

Likewise, most districts have some type of system, either formal or informal, whereby candidates are evaluated for performance. Obviously a new candidate for ministry won't have much of a track record, but there are ways of evaluating an individual through his or her local church. The church has seen the person day in and day out in many different situations. At least the district leader should ask the candidate's pastor, "Has Joe led people to Christ regularly?" "Does Jane demonstrate a ministry attitude in her church tasks?" "How effective is he with small groups?" "Does she lead people effectively?"

Evaluation for skill sets is similar in nature to the performance evaluation. It's an attempt to find out how a person has dealt with situations in the past. Both are built on the axiom that the best predictor of a person's future behavior is his or her past behavior. The skill evaluation is more focused on church planting behavioral skills. It requires an intensive investigation into a person's previous behavior, which would show possible patterns in responses to specific situations. This assessment is conducted by means of a behavioral interview.

So all three dimensions are addressed in the district as follows:

Assessment of	Performed by
Personality	Counseling Center
Performance	Recruitment process
Skills	Behavioral interview

The behavioral interview enables assessors to paint a picture of a candidate relative to the particular behaviors required for the task. The assessor paints a picture based on questions asked of the candidate. These questions ask for descriptions of how the person has behaved in previous circumstances, and the questions are keyed to specific behavioral dimensions. The assessors are not interested in how candidates felt but what they did. For this reason becoming an assessor may be difficult for some counselors. It requires a different set of skills than the reflective listening and empathic understanding common among counselors. The counselor might say, "How did that make you feel?" The behavioral assessor would say, "What did you do?" and, "Give me specific examples." Again, the best way to know how people will act in the future is to find out how they behaved in the past. It is the role of the assessor to identify and interpret a candidates behavior and match it against the church planter profile. It is imperative that assessors understand what behaviors are required for successful church planters. They need to know what particular behaviors they're looking for in the candidates.

While behavioral interviews are not new, applying them to church planter assessment is a relatively recent innovation. Charles Ridley of Indiana University has done the best work in applying the behavioral-interview technique to assessments. He has also done the only work in establishing behavioral dimensions required of successful church planters. We might consider him the guru of profile assessments. His involvement in establishing a PAS will ensure high quality at the outset. Let me take a moment to describe the PAS in capsule form and then expand on the process, training and benefits. Most districts will have neither the personnel nor the demand to establish a PAS on their own. For this reason nearby districts or other denominations may partner in the development of the PAS.

Working together may provide for better qualified assessors and more objective assessments. It also helps to share the cost of training and retraining.

The PAS is a multidenominational or multidistrict effort to ensure a quality, objective evaluation of church planting candidates, using the assessment process developed by Dr. Ridley. A number of benefits are readily apparent. Effectiveness in selecting church planters is greatly increased. The cost for quality assessments is reduced significantly. Accessibility to the process and the interviewers is convenient and immediate. The entire system is capable of being reproduced within denominations or partnering groups virtually anywhere.

In the Profile Assessment System a pool of 12-15 assessors is trained to use the behavioral interview technique in evaluating an individual relative to 15 performance dimensions. Dr. Ridley has determined that these performance dimensions are essential to successful church planters. While no one will be proficient in all of them equally, a candidate must demonstrate sufficient ability in enough of them to be recommended as a planter. There are five in particular that must be present. Any one of these five could be a "knock out" factor for the candidate, thereby eliminating him or her from any further consideration.

The assessor is trained to ask questions in such a way as to collect information about the candidate in each performance dimension. Two assessors conduct an interview that might last up to five hours. One of the assessors is from the sponsoring denomination. The other should be from another group in order to provide for objectivity.

In this way assessments can be conducted as needed and at the request of the district overseer. The system is both mobile and efficient. No setup is required and a career decision can be made almost immediately.

Early on in our experience with the PAS I called the designated contact person and told her I needed an assessment of a candidate within three weeks. I gave her the name and phone number and put it out of my mind. Less than three weeks later a three page, comprehensive evaluation was on my desk. It included a bottom line recommendation, strengths and weaknesses and an overall description of the candidate. That's not unusual. And believe me, it's a great help in making frequent decisions about church plants and the future of earnest servants.

Ideally the training of assessors should be conducted in an intensive setting over a period of three days. Dr. Ridley is the only qualified assessor trainer. Until he is able to provide other means, scheduling him for a training session must be done well in advance. His material and training is essential to the success of the PAS. The MMPI is administered to each assessor trainee. The results are sent to Dr. Ridley who may eliminate trainees should a red flag appear. This in effect is a personality evaluation of the assessor trainees themselves.

Subsequently, Dr. Ridley will provide in-depth training for the pool of assessors. This may include a fish-bowl evaluation in which he will actually conduct a behavioral interview of a church planter candidate while the trainees observe. In order to maintain quality control over such a system, assessors are certified in three categories: lead assessor, support assessor and candidate assessor.

It's imperative that a lead assessor be one of the two conducting each assessment in the system. Candidate assessors may observe the assessment interview but may not interview without further development

Once the training is complete, someone or a group will need to make logistical decisions regarding process, cost, coordination and communication. To help you understand how these issues can be dealt with, I'll simply describe the original system in Southern California. Yours may look a bit different depending on the partnering groups, demand and resources available to you. This pilot project included three categories of participants, each with specific roles and responsibilities: Chuck Ridley, denominational groups and Church Resource Ministries.

Dr. Ridley was responsible to provide training of the assessors using his validated performance dimensions and the behavioral interview process. He also provides certification of assessors and ongoing evaluation of the assessments in order to ensure quality.

CRM provided two assessors to be members of the pool of 15. This allows firsthand experience and involvement with the partnering denominations. Their primary role is to assist Dr. Ridley to organize future training sessions among other groups. They also provided expert guidance in defining the guidelines for operation of the PAS.

The denominational groups provide the bulk of the assessors. In this case, our Free Methodist District partnered with the Friends Church Southwest and the Missionary Church Western District to form the system. We have made the commitment to work together in assessing each other's candidates. Together we are responsible for administration of the system, coordinating interviews and meeting all quality control expectations we have agreed to.

Let me briefly run through the guidelines established by our Assessment Coordinating Team; Bob Logan served as a CRM representative on the team. At the group's request he wrote the initial draft designing the system. The team as a whole then modified and adapted the material and implemented the system using the following outline.

1. Prerequisites before scheduling behavioral interviews:

■ Candidates will be evaluated by the denominational leadership for suitability in character, doctrinal position and other denominational requirements.

■ Candidates and their spouses will be screened through a standardized psychological test. The specific instrument to be used in the assessment will be determined by the denominational group.

■ Candidates will be prescreened by appropriate denominational leader(s) to evaluate for visionizing capacity, intrinsic motivation, creating ownership and reaching the unchurched. These are the most critical performance dimensions. The prescreening ensures that assessments are being conducted on strong candidates only.

2. The candidate and his or her spouse will be interviewed together.

3. The interview will take at least four hours to complete.

4. One of the assessors will write the final report following the prescribed format. This format is given in the training session. In the event of a split decision, the report will discuss the rationale supporting the different conclusions. The report will be complete and returned to appropriate individuals within two weeks of the interview.

5. A copy of the final report will be sent to the sponsoring denomination, the assessors who conducted the interview and to the coordinating office. Communication of the evaluation to the candidate will be left to the denominational leaders.

6. Assessors will receive honoraria for their service. An additional amount will be charged to cover administrative costs and the cost of writing the evaluation.

7. Random auditing of an assessment interview/report will be conducted. The audit process asks the assessment team to back up its evaluations and subsequent conclusions with the specific behavioral data. The behavioral data includes the ratings on each performance dimension as well as the overall pattern of ratings. Monitoring the quality of the assessments may also include audio tapes of selected interviews and occasional personal observation by Dr. Ridley or his representative.

8. An assessment Coordinating Team will be appointed by the sponsoring denominations to oversee the system and handle adminis-

trative issues that may arise. Each denomination will select two representatives, including one assessor.

9. Nonsystem groups may request assessments with the understanding that the cost will be higher and that priority will be given to scheduling candidates of the sponsoring denominations.

The assessors are key to quality assessments. Carefully select persons to include in your pool for assessment training. They should be what Ridley calls "verbally rich." That is, they should be capable of accurately understanding and describing behavioral patterns. They should have strong interpersonal skills. Moreover, they should be highly tolerant and capable of remaining focused during the interview. Further, they should have personal experience of some type connected to church planting. This is to provide the emotional connection to the task. Most important, they should view their participation in the system as a ministry and understand how it fits into the total mission of the district.

I recall the genesis of our Profile Assessment System. It hadn't been a particularly good year in my district in the area of church planting. I had taken action to close three church planting projects. Each of those planters had hit bottom in his own way. We were able to redirect two of them into other ministries. The third wound up leaving the ministry entirely. In each case the conclusion was the same. The person planting the church was not a church planter. Each was a sincere, godly, motivated, Kingdom-minded person, just not a planter. My own confidence in selecting and deploying qualified planters was somewhat shaken.

So, I asked five other denominational leaders to discuss with me the idea of beginning an assessment system. Each of us had some experience with Ridley's profile assessment and believed it to be the best available. At the same time we were anxious to have a system or someone nearby, readily available and perhaps a bit less costly. It was not uncommon to spend $500 for travel alone to Indiana University for a Ridley evaluation. Church Resource Ministries, and specifically Logan, understood the district predicament represented in our group and worked with Ridley to agree to reproduce himself and ministry in a system.

Of the six leaders, two dropped out and the four who remained forged ahead with plans for a local, multidenominational, cost-effective, mobile, reproducible system that provided quick and quality evaluations as needed by each of us.

The first candidate I put through the PAS provided a classic example of its significance. Richard had come to me two years before and expressed interest in ministry, stating that God had called him to plant a church. He was a second-career candidate with a great deal of business and life experience. Over the course of two years Richard did everything I'd asked of him in an attempt to equip him. With no Bible training or seminary he enrolled in correspondence courses, read books, conducted interviews and attended seminars, all in an attempt to learn how to be a planter. Although there was some question regarding potential success, we thought Richard's motivation, life experience and calling would come through in the end. We proceeded with demographic studies, financial plans and public solicitation of prayer. Richard lined up supplemental employment, and I officially appointed him and his wife.

The PAS training occurred two weeks after his official appointment, and two weeks after that I requested an assessment. It was more to give the newly trained assessors some practice than to provide input for a deployment decision. Richard knew the assessment would be for information only. Once completed, I received the written evaluation and met with Richard to discuss it. Based on the data, the assessment recommended that he not be deployed. At the end of our meeting Richard asked: "If you had known this before making the decision to send me would you have made the same decision?" "No." I responded. As a result of the assessment and our meeting, Richard was redirected into a staff position where within weeks he was thrilled with the rewards of growth and new discoveries in ministry.

While in the case of Richard it was a difficult and emotional change of plans, we were able to avert a potentially disastrous and hurtful situation. Fortunately, with the PAS well established and operational, such a case should never occur. Every candidate for church planting is fully assessed as early as possible to avoid misplaced hopes, expectations and unwise decisions. If a candidate expresses interest in church planting, an assessment early on will ensure that you are investing resources in qualified planters.

There is nothing wrong with not being suited as a church planter. There is a great deal wrong with selecting someone who is not suited to plant a church. The resulting hurt, grief, frustration and burnout can undermine the very call of God in the lives of many sincere and zealous individuals, to say nothing of their families. The PAS is the best investment you can make to avoid this unnecessary waste of potential.

New Church Incubator

*Provides a supportive environment,
skill training and coaching relationships for
planters, their spouses and key lay leaders
from conception through the first year
after public worship.*

If the PCN represents the primary paradigms of a church planting system and if the PAS represents the most immediate results for the district planting enterprise, the New Church Incubator (NCI) represents the best direct resource for church planters. The NCI has the longest tenure of experience as a church planting component. It was developed by Church Resource Ministries' Bob Logan and Steve Ogne. The Western District of the Missionary Church provided the funds for development and the planters for field testing the concept.

The NCI provides a warm, supportive environment for planters, spouses and lay leaders. It assists in the development of new churches from conception through the first year after birth. The NCI recognizes critical points of need for the church planter who is considering deployment. Some notable points addressed by the NCI are: 1) prayer partner support and how to develop it; 2) conception of the vision and how to shape and focus it; 3) planning the birth and how to mobilize seed families; 4) opening day and how to prepare for a relevant start.

A key ingredient to the NCI, which should be attractive to any district leader, is the accountability and support of planters. It seems that every district that has attempted to start churches at some point finds itself unable to provide the kind of support uniquely required by planters.

As with the PCN, the NCI has monthly meetings led by the facilitator. It's important that as you select your facilitator and send him or her for training you understand clearly the importance of this role. He or she must have some direct experience in church planting and command the respect of your planters. Don't pick someone just because he or she chairs the Church Growth Committee of your district. A proven record of success in growth and planting is needed. He or she will guide the group of planters through the process of preparation for deployment. This process starts with nurturing the vision. In its infancy the vision of a church planter is a delicate thing that can easily be squashed if it is not nurtured. What the fledgling planter needs is a cocoon or womb in which his or her ideas can grow strong with affirmation and guidance provided by a primary care giver. Further, the presence of others in a similar status only serves to fuel the growth. Sit with a group of planters and watch the synergy of creative thinking and support unfold. The monthly NCI meetings are as critical to the long-term health of the new church as prenatal care is to a child.

My Italian grandmother had 12 children in Sicily. Six of them survived. When I ask my father why so many died, the answer is simply: "They didn't have the prenatal care we have now." New life is delicate and requires nurture from conception through maturity. The fledgling vision and development of planters is essential to successful church planting. It's a terrible thing to waste. The process developed by Logan and Ogne for the NCI is well thought through, comprehensive and progressive. It provides the best possible environment for God to nurture His call in the planter couple through natural steps toward healthful birth and growth.

As crucial as the monthly meetings are, the monthly coaching appointments are possibly more important. These fall midway between the NCI meetings. In effect, then, the planter has direct, focused contact with a group or individual approximately every two weeks. The coach attends the NCI meetings and is able to hold the planter accountable to assignments. They also are able to troubleshoot in the particular circumstances of his or her planter. Don't underestimate this role. It is absolutely essential and may mean the difference between success and failure for a planter. Think carefully and make wise selections of your coaches. Also be careful not to overload the coaches. They are probably successful and busy pastors. You want their expertise and experience. But you don't want to break them with too much to do.

The NCI makes use of its own material, the *Church Planter's Toolkit* and Logan's book, *Beyond Church Growth*. Your planters will have regular care and the best resources available, all provided by a trained facilitator and coaches who are fully focused on them. Believe me, you can't do better yourself, leader. Providing this type of resource is the best investment you can make in their success.

Once you've identified your facilitator and coaches, let someone else give you an opinion regarding your choices. Maybe it's another overseer or parachurch resource person. Whoever it is, make sure he or she's had experience with the NCI and knows what's required. He or she will tell you if you've chosen the right people. Then take your team to the training event. Similar to the PCN, the training is conducted in two days by Logan and Ogne. It's designed specifically to equip your oversight team.

Overseer, you may be tempted to send your people to these training events. Don't yield to that temptation. You need the exposure and you need to be seen there. Your team needs to have your presence, and your constituency needs to know your seriousness regarding church planting. This is true of the training for each of the other components as well. Be there. It is your business. Your people want you there.

At the NCI training you and your team will learn effective coaching techniques, how to plan strategically for church planting in your district and how to get an NCI going. The NCI itself will become the method by which you and your team can provide a supportive environment for church planting. It will do so through skill training, prayer, networking and relationships, coaching and defining strategies to implement the vision of church planters.

As I've already said, the NCI along with the PCN and the PAS constitute the three essential components of any system (Figure 4). The PCN deals exclusively with the parent church. The PAS deals with the planter. The NCI is the component that deals exclusively with preparation for birth from the church planter's perspective. It certainly builds upon the foundations of parent preparation in the PCN. It is also dependent on the quality of screening provided by the PAS. In the NCI, for the first time, the center of attention is the future new church itself.

Currently there are dozens of New Church Incubators in operation around the United States and Canada. Great success has accompanied this compo-

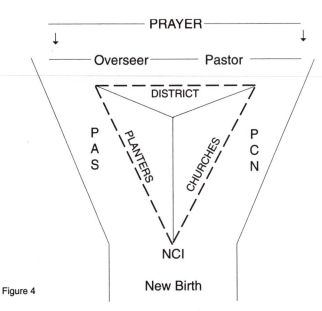

Figure 4

nent. While it is a major step forward in church planting, don't make the mistake of thinking an NCI is all you need to make your district a church planting movement. It is fully effective only when implemented with the other components, especially the Parent Church Network and the Profile Assessment System.

Because the NCI primarily resources the church planter, I'd like to digress a moment to comment briefly about them. Through involvement in church planting as an observer, planter, parent pastor and overseer, I've come to understand a few facts about planters and how to affirm them.

1. They need more than money. They need support and connection. Qualified planters probably won't be too concerned about needing to raise some of their own financial support. For catalytic entrepreneurs it's no big deal. Don't misunderstand, they need your financial help. Just don't think that money fulfills the

district obligation to them. They need to know people are with them, especially at critical points.

2. Church planters believe what you tell them so be careful what you say. They'll take your word at face value. If you suggest a "possibility" of funds or equipment, it's a done deal in planters' minds. They'll hang a lot of hope on what you intend only as a suggestion. Potentially it will set them up for major disappointment when you are unable to deliver on your idea.

3. Integrity is high, therefore careful representation of the district and denomination is essential. The personality of planters tends to give them a strong sense of right and wrong. The lines defining issues — theological, social, lifestyle — are bold and unwavering. So where your district or denomination may have expectations planters will do everything in their power to respect them. They may do so even to a greater degree than you believe necessary. Other pastors may have more moderate attitudes toward those expectations than the planters do. If, then, denominational expectations are described in legalistic, exclusivistic terms, planters will be thrown into turmoil as they attempt to fulfill the burning desire to reach people while maintaining integrity with the denominational expectation.

4. Planters are thoroughbreds. They need their head. They are the embodiment of movement. Every district needs people like them to keep pushing ahead. Attempting to harness planters too tightly is really asking them to become something they're not. The very characteristic that makes them effective planters is the characteristic that, if checked, will cause failure. They are intrinsically motivated and catalytic people. They are the kind of person who, with liberal reign, will score in church planting.

5. They require high flexibility regarding the institution. This is closely related to number 4. Remember, unencumbered by historical baggage, planters are the epitome of pure movement. They provide proper balance to the human tendency toward institutionalism. You must carefully interpret the institution to them and in some cases make room to accommodate their raw energy. A policy or procedure you've grown up with may need to be adjusted or stretched for them. That leaves you open to others who may cry "foul" or "unfair," but that's your lot as a leader.

6. We must stand with them. They're our marines. You cannot reserve support until after they have a church of 500. They need to know you're with them even before they hit the beaches. Sure, they may do things in unorthodox ways, but you can judge their character and commitment to your district team and then throw your unwavering support behind them before they are even deployed. Trust their character and relationship to the district. They won't embarrass you or misrepresent the core values of your denominational identity. What they do may look a little different from what a majority of your pastors would do. Of course, how many of your pastors could do what you're asking these to do?

As you now understand, these first three components are essential to your system. Because of the critical role they play in the Century 21 System I've attempted to provide a relatively comprehensive understanding of each of them without including actual material. I'll attempt to be briefer with the other seven components. In some cases there is similar curriculum and structure. In others the structure is looser and more dependent upon district procedures and personality. A couple of the components, particularly the

Strategic Planning Network and the Meta-Church Network, could be stand-alone components that operate to the benefit of local churches but quite apart from a church planting effort. They greatly strengthen the system, however, and so are included as significant contributors. Let's continue with a summary description of the other components to the Century 21 Church Planting System.

Recruitment Network

Establishes an intentional strategy for recruiting a pool of pastoral candidates particularly focusing on those with church planting interest and proficiency.

Recruitment is, perhaps, the most important of any district priority. As you know, leadership is the single most important factor in the success or failure of an organization. (See chapter 2.) If your district is not constantly recruiting leaders and strengthening the leadership team, it will eventually deteriorate. The most important task for the overseer is recruitment. Constantly adding strong leaders to the district team will provide for an increasingly bright future. It's not surprising, then, that the recruitment of planting candidates is essential to the success of the system and ultimately the church planting enterprise.

It's very important for overseers to understand that we cannot develop a pool of planters. The pool that you want to develop is a pool of ministerial candidates from which you will be able to identify prospective planters. I've heard many overseers ask and I myself have asked, "Where can I get a church planter?" The answer is simple. You find planters in the pool of candidates you have developed in your regular recruitment network. The key, then, is not to go looking for planters but to enhance and expand your network that already is in place. Further, add an emphasis to your network that focuses on church planting. Your goal is to identify candidates in your general network who have a germinal interest in planting. Once someone tells the district that they have an interest in church planting the overseer can guide them into the system. In this way the district can shape and train its own planters.

The Recruitment Network, therefore, is a tailor-made plan to increase the system of identifying candidates in the district by means of strategies and events that will increase the pool of ministerial candidates while integrating a church planting dimension. This dimension will act as a trigger for those within the pool who have a fledgling interest in planting. Once the trigger is set off and interest is expressed, the system will provide the way to explore that interest and possibly confirm it. That's the goal of a Recruitment Network.

So, you see, the Recruitment Network is largely dependent on the individual district and overseer. If your church planting system is in place and if your recruitment is infected by the overseer's personal vision for church planting, which will serve as the trigger for potential planters, it only remains intentionally to expand the size of the farm system or pool.

Most districts have addressed this through the establishment of events that highlight full-time ministry as a calling. For example, you might consider a Lord of the Harvest Banquet. This type of annual event uses the network of churches already in place within the district. Additionally it leverages the local pastor to live out the inherent desire within every pastor to reproduce himself or herself.

Notify the district pastors of the plan and solicit their support in prayer and participation. Ask that they pray for guidance to identify individuals within their congregations who may be considering a call to ministry. Maybe the pastor, through prayer, has a sense of discernment regarding someone. Those are the people you want. The local pastor is in the best position to observe the gifts, talents and work of the Spirit in his or her people's lives. Trust the pastor's judgment.

Ask the pastors to bring those people to a district event designed especially for them. At the event provide an attractive setting. Cater the event or do it at a nice banquet facility. This may be the most important event in the lives of some of those in attendance. It certainly represents the future of the district, so don't be afraid to make it nice. Potluck won't do.

Prepare a quality program, but not too long. Challenge the people with district vision, the need for pastoral leadership, church planting dreams and Scripture-based definition of a call to ministry. Include a brief testimony from a respected and successful pastor. Preferably this should be a planter. Notice how you can gently interweave the planting priority to provide the trigger. Ideally a brief video, slides or personal testimonies can give the prospective candidates a feel for the larger work in the district.

Finally, provide opportunity for those in attendance to express interest. This is not a decision they will make in one evening so don't expect it. Simply give them opportunity to fill out a card indicating interest in exploring ministry, or church planting in particular, as a calling. These are the people you need to keep close to. Do it through letters, personal contact, events and especially through their pastor.

This event can be vital to the future of the district. In it you are expanding the pool of pastoral candidates and planting candidates. Don't shortchange this priority. Keep it sharp, focused, brief, high quality and pay for it. This is a cost the district needs to assume fully. Not the local church and especially not the prospects.

Another idea in putting together a Recruitment Network is the Institute for Lay Training developed by the Nazarenes in Canada. Although it resembles a Pastor Factory, its motivating force is the identification of new candidates who are primarily second-career people.

Marjorie Osborne is Director of Church Planting for the Church or the Nazarene in Canada. She tested the concept during an intensive planting effort in Toronto between 1988 and 1992, from which 28 churches were started. Obviously new churches can't be started without leaders and the first place to look for planters is the lay membership in existing churches. The ILT provides eight courses designed for lay persons in eight weekend sessions. Each of the eight sessions provides 12 contact hours, and they are spread over 12 months. The classes are taught at an existing church in the region by respected teachers with practical experience. They were designed to give participants special focus on evangelistic growth and an entry point for continued preparation toward ministry and possibly church planting. The initial goal for the ILT was 20 students. Thirty-two actually participated with more than 50 percent continuing into ministry. Some of the courses taught are: Bring Them In (Gathering a Group

Together); TLC (Basics of Pastoral Care); Growing Up in Christ (Individual and Corporate Discipleship). The ILT was such a success in "Target Toronto" that it has been replicated in other cities for the purpose of recruitment. It is a natural feeder for the ongoing ministry preparation track of the denomination.

In planning these events, you will find that if they are future-oriented, mission-driven and attractive, a majority of those who participate will be from churches in your church planting system. They will come from churches in the Parent Church Network, Meta-Church Network, Strategic Planning Network and Maturing Church Cluster. These are the churches that are creating movement and movement creates ever-broadening ripples. They must begin producing their own planters if they are truly to become reproducing churches. The natural result of churches focused on mission is the production of people who want to be part of the mission as a calling. And remember, mission-driven churches attract mission-minded people and produce mission-driven leaders.

Pastor Factory

*Trains proven lay leaders to become founding
pastors and lifelong learners
through internship, mentoring and biblical
study with small-group interaction.*

The concept of a pastor factory was first used by Don Stuart of Hope Chapel in Southern California. The idea is being developed into a reproducible system by Neil Cole and Bob Logan. Although terms and titles may change as further refinements are made, the Pastor Factory refers to a well-defined system in the local church environment whereby church leaders are produced for church planting, pastoring, missions or lay leadership. This component is very closely related to the Recruitment Network and can be one method of fulfilling its intent as well.

In the case where one church does not have enough people to form an operational system, the Pastor Factory (PF) allows for regional, multichurch participation. Ten to twelve individuals with leadership potential work with a facilitator through the prescribed curriculum. The ideal environment for the Pastor Factory process is a cell-based church where people are already in small-group-leadership positions. In this context candidates for the PF can most easily be identified. They will be the ones who are effectively leading small groups in reproducing themselves and assimilating new believers. The PF can help these people consider a call to ministry.

Program-based churches may also benefit from the PF process. For it to be effective, however, they must have a strong desire to become cell-based or at least have subsections of the church that are highly focused on mission. In these churches it will be more difficult to spot the potential candidates.

In any case, the kind of people who qualify for participation in the PF meet the following criteria articulated by Cole.

- Those who sense a call to ministry but have not received either a high school diploma or an undergraduate degree and are not in a position in life to acquire one.
- Those who are called to minister to a people group that is far removed from the seminary culture and yet need thorough training that will not divorce them from their context of ministry.
- Those who sense a call to full-time ministry while in the midst of a career. Because of their place in life and the demands of supporting a family, it is not feasible for them to enter seminary, yet they need adequate training for their new career.
- Lay men and women who desire preparation for the ministry but are not able to invest in a graduate-level education.
- Visionaries who have an entrepreneurial spirit and gifts of leadership, but have found that they lack the academic skills necessary to fulfill seminary requirements.

The primary goal of the Pastor Factory is to raise up and prepare church planters. As we discussed in the section on the Recruitment Network, however, when attempting to develop planters a percentage of the candidates will be redirected to other areas of ministry. This may include missions, teaching, pastoring or lay leadership. Because of this natural vectoring of candidates based on call, skill, gift mix and need, a secondary goal of the PF is to develop church leaders for these various areas of ministry. There will be a natural increase in the quality and number of people moving into these ministries as well.

The Pastor Factory (Figure 5) is divided into two general stages — the Leadership Training System (LTS) and the Pastor Factory Network (PFN). The LTS is essentially an informal discipleship process whereby a pastor may invest in individuals whom he or she determines to have particular promise for leadership in ministry. It consists of one-on-one mentoring during which the pastor may guide candidates through the steps of development to the point where they commit to the more formal PFN. The LTS allows the pastor to start with individuals at their current level of understanding. By the time a commitment to the second stage is made a relatively common level of development should be present in all of the candidates. As Pastor Cole says, "The LTS participant is not always aware of the systematic way I'm leading them. In some cases they just think the pastor is an incredibly discerning person who always has just what they need at various stages in their development."

At the middle point of the Pastor Factory some individuals are redirected into increased lay leadership, others into staff ministry. Those who proceed to the second stage do so after a full assessment is performed by the Profile Assessment System and a positive recommendation is given.

While stage I (LTS) emphasizes skill training, stage II (PFN) emphasizes cognitive theological education. For some denominations this will meet all requirements for ordination or licensure. For others it will be complementary.

Stage II allows the candidate to gain basic theological education while developing a planting proposal and identifying a core of seed families. The facilitator and local pastor become the primary resource persons in this more formal and structured stage.

Upon completion of Stage II, the candidate should continue in the New Church Incubator. Ideally by this point the candidate will have attended the Church Planters' Summit. If not, it should precede involvement in the NCI. If the candidate's church is a participant in the Parent Church Network, the parent church will be undergoing simultaneous preparation.

The Pastor Factory Process

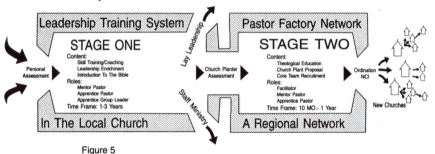

Figure 5

Because the Pastor Factory emphasizes hands-on training with a focus on reproducing groups, it's an excellent partner with the Meta-Church Network (MCN). Churches participating in the MCN are prime candidates for a Pastor Factory. Conversely, churches committed to beginning a PF are poised for effective transition to the meta model with the help of the MCN.

Church Planters' Summit

*A retreat designed to orient
church planters with the Century 21 Church
Planting System and its motivating philosophy
within the district or regional context. (Moore)*

Most districts active in church planting have attempted something like the Church Planters' Summit (CPS) in various forms. Often it has simply been a get-together for brainstorming and idea sharing. In some cases it has resulted in more regular meetings of regional planters. The weakness of these previous efforts is that they have not identified a clear focus with objectives for the event. Frequently too much is expected. Little of really long-term value results. We expect that relational bonding, accountability, skill training, trouble shooting and motivation will all be achieved. The result is a nice gathering with good feelings but with little direction.

Usually when people gather without clear goals, the focus tends to become negatively slanted. I recall a period when we gathered our planters without really outlining a strategy. It wound up becoming an encounter group for problem situations as one after the other unloaded emotional burdens for the others to share. Obviously there's nothing wrong with such a process except when it becomes the primary focus of the group to the exclusion of developmental objectives. The atmosphere of the group takes on a quasi martyr dynamic with a "downer" feeling. At its extreme it can deteriorate into commiseration over the woes and burdens of church planting.

This is by no means an intentional process. It just happens to highly task oriented people who many times are frustrated with unrealized goals or timelines. The answer is not to eliminate this type of forum. Each of us needs an outlet for this pressure. Rather, we need to add a proactive, controlled strategy for keeping balance in the group, balance between burden-sharing, strategic thinking and skill training. Enter the CPS, which sets the stage in the planter's mind for the rest of his or her experience in the system.

The CPS is formatted in a two to three day event as often as needed to initiate new planter candidates. Planters and their spouses are able to be guided in laying the planks of their platform that will launch and frame their efforts. The CPS is intentionally designed to provide careful balance between the public and private dimensions of planting. The private or unseen dimension would include prayer, relationships and accountability. The public or seen dimension includes strategy, systems and training. The idea is that these dimensions will provide guidance, framing and a pattern for the planter's ongoing development and activity.

Tweed Moore, a member of our district team, was assigned as point man to develop the CPS. He illustrated the six elements in a hand diagram (Figure 6).

The three elements I've identified as private or unseen are directly connected to the personality or identity of the planter. These will serve as stabilizers in rough times much as the bottom of an iceberg keeps it stable in rough seas.

Figure 6

The key element or leveling force in this unseen dimension is prayer (Figure 7).

Conversely the three public or seen elements deal with the program or plan of the planter. They become the visible elements to which people relate. This is the tangible, public dimension, which must be well developed in the planter's mind before launching. The key or leveling element in this dimension is strategy.

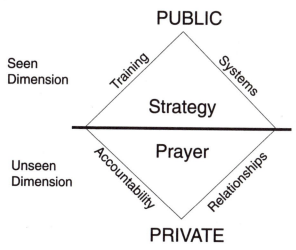

Figure 7

Let me briefly describe the elements of each dimension and how they are developed at the CPS.

Unseen

1. Prayer — Obviously no effort to expand the Kingdom will succeed without total saturation in prayer. The planter will be called upon to develop a prayer team in the NCI as will the parent church in the PCN. The CPS helps the planter understand the priority of prayer in the project. The role of prayer warriors

in providing a backdrop of sending/blessing prayer is explained as is the importance of listening/directional prayer on the part of the planter.

2. Accountability — Each denomination has its own accountability for pastors through credentialing. There is probably similar accountability for new plants in the process of becoming churches. In our case the progression is from Planting Project to Fellowship to Society (a term originating in the Methodist revival). These are outlined in detail to the planters so that they understand their denominational family's process. Additionally the points of accountability within the Century 21 System are carefully explained. Accountability among the participants of the CPS develops informally as relationships develop around a common interest.

3. Relationships — Increasingly, districts draw candidates from other denominations or districts. You cannot, therefore, assume that everyone knows everyone else. Even if all come from the same district, the commonality of church planting provides windows of insight into people that perhaps were never known. In any case, this group of people will begin to bond relationally very quickly. This will provide a rich environment for dialogue and sharing. Additionally, it will ensure the highest success of other component parts when these same people participate together in the NCI, or New Church Network, or eventually the Meta-Church Network.

Seen

1. Strategy — This is the key to the activities in which the planters engage. The CPS helps them begin the process of developing core values that will govern

their plans. The planters are guided in developing a mission statement and begin general planning for their new church.

2. Training — Although it won't be comprehensive, a brief overview of the planting process is provided to guide the planters. It is further developed in the NCI. The CPS provides some basic handholds for the developing planter's thoughts.

3. Systems — The new planters may not conceive of all that lies ahead. Neither will they be aware of the resources available to them throughout their work. At the CPS denominational vision and resources are explained. Most important the CPS facilitator helps planters comprehend the Century 21 System and how they will flow through it. It gives planters a bird's eye view. The result is high confidence and affirmation that they will not simply be dropped off at the end of the world and left to fend for themselves. This is particularly important to spouses. This element assures planters that they are important. A lot of effort has gone into assuring their success. Believe me, they'll notice and appreciate it.

The CPS is a prerequisite to the NCI and to launching a plant. Additionally, it is imperative that candidates receive a recommendation, or at least a mixed rating, from their assessment in the PAS. These requirements will ensure a quality CPS and an effective NCI.

Maturing Church Cluster

*Assists new churches in the first five years
to identify and navigate the major paradigm
shifts required in maturing into a
healthy and growing church.*

The Maturing Church Cluster (MCC) is still in developmental stages. Our district is developing material. And the Church Resource Ministries is developing a New Church Network which is currently being piloted. In whatever form, a MCC will play a significant role in shaping the future of a church much as the CPS and NCI shape the future of a planter. What a new church is able to assimilate as core values and priorities will guide its activity for the rest of its existence. As a child's personality is imprinted in its earliest years, so also a church's personality and focus is permanently ingrained in the first five years of its life.

This window of molding and shaping a church's personality closes quickly after its first few years. It is important, then, to affect it in a way that will keep it mission-driven and reproduction-minded. Further, with each year of life a new church grows less and less dependent on the singular leadership of the planter. This is a natural process that is healthful. Yet the less influence a catalytic planter has the more important it becomes to keep the new church focused. The alternative is to watch an enthusiastic new plant become a stale, stagnant institution when it should be experiencing the prime of life. There are actually new churches which at age 5 or 6 are acting like churches of 70 or 80 years.

Because the NCI carries a new church through its first year after birth, the Maturing Church Cluster will pick up at approximately that time. There will be some overlap of time and focus between the NCI and the MCC. Generally, however, the MCC emphasizes the issues relevant to the natural maturing process of a young church. They include organizational structure, staffing for growth, releasing ministry to laity, role and nature of pastoral leadership and maturity steps of a developing church.

One of the most difficult aspects of new church maturity is the radical shift of identity required by the congregation and pastor. For all of its life, the new congregation has been happy as a group of people enthusiastic about the novelty of new life and the freshness of creating their own church. There comes a point in the first few years when the novelty wears off and the people realize that this is their church. Ownership in the laity begins to surface. They begin to see that their new church has a future consisting of more than just one Sunday celebration after another. It becomes their family. They see their increasing responsibility and role. It becomes something they want to pass on to their children. The corporate mind is jelling and the multigenerational identity is emerging. The need for lay ministry-driven structures and attitudes must be addressed in order to fuel the continuing maturing process. This is a significant rite of passage in every new church. The MCC guides the pastor and lay leaders in navigating this transition.

Similarly, the role of the planter must change. At birth, the planter must be catalytic, entrepreneurial and highly focused to launch the project. In the early years of life, however, that role broadens. For someone who is accustomed to making unilateral decisions with little or no consultation it can be difficult to allow others into the process. The planter has been solely responsible for strategy and procedures, philosophy of ministry and mission. Now the fruit of their labor — the people — must be included.

As the church grows, more people need to be discipled into leadership which means the pastor allows their involvement and influence. Additionally, the complexity of leading an ever-expanding ministry is multiplied. It's no longer a matter of single-minded, catalytic energy motivated by one goal. It becomes a multifaceted task. Legal contracts, disgruntled people, long-term discipleship, community relationships, to name only a few, now introduce themselves into the pastor's portfolio. All of this demands that a catalytic planter undergo radical rewiring to become a pastor/leader. The frustration is increased as the pastor feels he or she is losing the very thing which he or she cherished and made him or her successful — intense, mission-driven focus on unsaved or unchurched people.

In reality the planter need not lose this distinctive. It simply must be repackaged and redeveloped to accommodate the maturing church. This is a critical point for the planters. If they successfully undergo this rewiring, all is well, and dynamic ministry growth happens. If, however, the transition is too much and the planters are unable to make it, the growth of the church is capped, premature aging sets in and the personality of the church is cemented before it has fully blossomed. In this case the district overseer needs to be ready to make a change in order to let the church develop and in order to get the planters back into a context where their gifts are not frustrated. If planters cannot make this shift, asking them to do so will be asking them to become someone they haven't the capacity to be.

They'll shut down or burn out. Don't force it. Be sensitive to the possibility that it can't happen.

Not long ago I received a phone call from Marty, one of my pastors. It was late at night and I knew quickly all was not well. For some time he had shared that the pressure was mounting and he was not entirely sure how to respond. His church was 3 years old. Explosive growth had occurred. Frequently Marty referred to his church as a crowd that he was trying to develop into a congregation. Fear continued to mount as he realized how much pressure was on him to perform and keep the momentum up. Occasionally a panic attack would strike, debilitating this gifted man. Marty gave his associate instructions to carry a sermon with him every Sunday and be prepared to preach with no advance notice except to be called forward and introduced as the speaker of the day.

That late Tuesday night Marty had come to the end. He realized it when he knelt in front of his wife and asked for her prayer, as he had often done. This time, however, her response was, "I can't. I just don't have any more to give." A cold fear gripped my friend as his ultimate crutch was knocked out from under him. He called and said, "I'm at the end and I don't know what to do."

Marty had tried counseling, prayer intervention, intense searching for unconfessed sin, physical exercise and diet adjustments. Now he faced a wall. We both knew it was critical and his very survival as a minister was on the line. He was totally flat and needed someone to tell him what his next step should be. It had to be immediate and decisive. That night we laid general plans for a three-month sabbatical to commence that weekend. I scheduled a meeting with the church leaders and set in motion a chain of events to assist the church and pastor through a major transition of development. Probably the most important thing Marty heard that night was, "Plan to take three months off and don't concern yourself with the church. It'll be okay."

Marty didn't preach that Sunday. He read a letter we had talked over and began his rewiring. Over the course of the next three months he rested, played, read, studied, interviewed pastors, went to counseling and journaled. It was an amazing sight to see a new man emerge. Confidence, enthusiasm, joy, creativity and command returned. One of the most obvious manifestations of his new focus — he was in charge, not just everybody's friend. Spontaneous vulnerability gave way to intentional, guarded, on-purpose attitudes. While it required discipline, it was a relief. He continues to grow in this new identity.

At the same time the church had to face its own identity crisis. It was no longer a happy, partying group of people who watched the leader carry the burden. New leaders had to emerge. The church made sobering decisions. It wasn't easy as the people were called upon to define their church with their pastor *in absentia*. Who are we? What's our mission? What's our role? Privilege now proved to have an alter ego — responsibility.

My task was to help both pastor and people through a major life gate. The people had to realize that the pastor who would show up in three months would be different. Not a planter but a strategic leader. Likewise, Marty needed to know the church to which he would return was already different. They were growing up.

They wouldn't do something just because he said to. This was now their church, not just his.

Within six months of Marty's return nearly the entire staff was new. The structure was reconfigured and whole new echelons of lay leaders surfaced. Today the church is healthier than ever. It is a mature, responsible congregation that understands commitment, leadership, identity and corporate maturity. Sure, there are still many growing pains but it's no longer a child. It's a young adult with unfathomable potential.

This is only one brief example of the paradigm shifts and identity transition required of every new church early in its history. This one was successful. Not every one is so blessed. Is it wise to let this transition happen and hope everything works out? Can we assume that the pastor will call the district overseer for help? Will the overseer always be able to provide the right guidance? Should we wait for the critical "Tuesday night call?" I don't think so. If there is a way to guide a new church through this kind of developmental step before the crisis hits, we'd better use it. The Maturing Church Cluster gives the district that option for the good growth of new churches.

Strategic Planning Network

*Networks pastors and lay leaders in
diagnosing and planning to lead their churches
in breaking growth barriers and developing
a commitment to start a new church.*

Often local churches succumb to the ever-present temptation to protect themselves and become institutionalized. The mission becomes diffused and is reframed in terms that justify self-centered preservation. We've all seen it. The question is, do we recognize it? Or better yet, will we do something about it?

Don't allow anyone to suggest that you simply write off these plateaued existing churches. Although it is said church planting may represent 80 percent of a district's growth, existing churches may represent at least 80 percent of the district's capacity to plant churches. Think of the resources and where they come from; think of the heritage that provides richness; think of the pool of ministerial candidates; and, mostly, think of the pool of prospective parent churches. No doubt, existing churches — plateaued or growing — represent potential for growth and planting. They're worth investing in.

It's imperative in this section that you understand a basic truth about redirecting and revitalizing local churches. Do you remember our discussion in chapter 2 about the importance of district leadership in becoming a church planting movement? Well, apply those principles to the local church and the role of the pastor. If the pastor is not involved, leading and committed to the revitalizing process, it won't happen. Why? Because the church rises and falls on leadership.

Because this is true, any effort in strategically positioning local churches for growth and reproduction will demand attention to "leadership formation." This term applies to an intricate integration of Leadership Development and Spiritual Formation. I'll leave the exhaustive treatment of leadership formation to a later work. Suffice it to say that district leadership must address this in some way in order to effect successful renewal in the local church.

Some Strategic Planning Network (SPN) programs incorporate some form of this element into the regular process. A more effective way to address leadership formation is for the district overseer to take personal responsibility for this dimension in the total ministry he or she has with all pastors under his or her care. Such is our case.

For many years I have held leadership formation at the identity level to be the single most important issue among church leaders. Because of that priority I have attempted to use every circumstance in our district — corporate and individual — as a teaching moment to drive home this point. Our identity must be shaped in being before we can truly succeed in doing. I attribute many moral failures, cases of burnout and stress in the ministry to a lack of understanding proper identity in spiritual leadership. The result is ministry activities motivated by the need to perform successfully and achieve statistical results.

So in addition to using district gatherings and one-on-one meetings with pastors to address this priority, I've resourced my people with others who ring the same bell — Richard Foster, Dallas Willard, David McKenna, Sam Kamaleson, to name a few. In this way the total district awareness has been sensitized to the issues of leadership identity, which thereby provides a healthful context for effective participation in the SPN. Whether you address this agenda on a district level or within the process of your SPN is not so important as the fact that you address it in some way.

The objectives of the SPN are twofold:
1) To assist the local church in breaking its growth barriers and restoring health; and
2) To bring a local church to a condition where it may commit to reproducing itself in a new congregation.

In a church that is diffused, flat, lifeless, the first phase to becoming refocused is purely diagnostic. Before the doctor can prescribe correction, a diagnosis is required. It's not enough to know that health is missing. We must understand why there is no healthful growth. Only then are we able to apply the appropriate corrective action to bring the church back to vitality. Only a vital, healthy church has the ability to reproduce. Ill health in a church always brings infertility.

This diagnostic element of redirecting a church is of primary concern to the SPN. A significant amount of time and energy is spent in this element. A group of five to 12 churches are clustered together and become diagnostic consultants to one another within the parameters of the SPN. Tools developed by other organizations, such as the diagnostic self test provided through Fuller Institute, become the means for the facilitator to guide each church in understanding its ailment. Each pastor and lay team is asked to conduct this self study. Each team in turn then makes the information available to the total group. Under the guidance of the facilitator each church receives input from the others in this diagnostic procedure. For those teams not being diagnosed in a particular meeting this becomes an exercise in sensitivity to the obstacles and symptoms of plateaued or unhealthy churches.

Once diagnoses are given the SPN moves into its second phase — prescription. It's important to note that no two churches are alike and no two conditions are alike. Therefore, it is imperative that the facilitator guide the group in applying prescriptive, corrective action individually. Seeing this happen in a group reminds each team of the individuality of its church.

Have you ever noticed how churches seeking help for growth tend to assume that "what works for church X will work for us"? They proceed to import and impose someone else's program without regard for the individuality of their church and the uniqueness of their condition. Perhaps this occurs because a) churches try to heal themselves without outside help and b) they do so in a vacuum, which causes people to assume that every church is alike. The constant presence of other churches in the SPN forces attention to individuality.

When church leaders finally come face-to-face with the uniqueness of their own circumstances, they will be able to understand the transcendent principles on which they must focus. Put another way, if we don't understand the individual nature of the church, we'll not be able to differentiate between "principle" and "program." We'll spend all our time implementing someone else's program without comprehending the principle that drives it. Once principles are grasped, tailor-made prescriptive programs can be applied to the good of one particular church. Usually it's the leaders of diffused or unfocused churches who most need to understand this difference. Expecting them to do so on their own is asking too much and is unrealistic. The SPN is designed to help with this insight.

Additionally, once a strategy has been laid out by the church leadership team, the SPN acts as an accountability group in holding the team to task. Regular progress reports are measured against the prescribed strategy by the other SPN participants. This type of peer accountability is far better than what one overseer may be able to provide. Here again, allowing groups of churches to work together with common goals provides a natural reproducible system that builds skill, accountability and relationships — the goal of every district overseer. Efforts are multiplied and potential results are unlimited.

Ray Ellis and Dan Reeves have developed a specific process that meets the expectations of the SPN. They call it the Cluster Catalyzing Consultation (CCC). The purpose of the CCC is to assist small and medium size churches in becoming redirected, refocused, revitalized resulting in growth and reproduction.

The process involves clustering pastors and lay leaders of five to 12 churches together nine times in a 12-month period with the option of extending the cluster for another 12 months. A certified church growth consultant assigned by Ellis and Reeves facilitates each of these cluster meetings. Particular emphasis is placed on equipping the pastor to integrate the consulting and planning principles into his or her church. Additionally, key district leaders are trained to begin other clusters through ongoing coaching by the consultants. The total CCC process includes three phases.

Phase I — Diagnostic Analysis. This phase involves the pastor and his team in use of the latest analytical tools to assess their local church. More important, it brings the expertise of the consultant and the insight of the other cluster participants to bear to assist the pastor to interpret and apply the results. The resulting work becomes the primary planning document for the rest of the process.

Phase II — Master Planning. This phase builds on the diagnostic, planning document to formulate a comprehensive plan to address the specific needs of the church. Under the oversight of the consultant and in the context of the cluster, the pastor and team apply the principles they are discovering to a tailor-made growth plan.

Phase III — Accountability Checkpoints. This phase is perhaps the most valuable in that it assists the pastor to stay on task. Based on the planning document and the master plan, the consultant and group review progress and assist in refocusing priorities and targets.

The genius of the Cluster Catalyzing Consultation is its focus on involving the pastor and lay leaders to do their own diagnosing, planning and implementing. With direction given by the consultant within the group setting, the CCC is a valuable process. Each participating church pays a small fee that includes the consultant's expense and makes the CCC an affordable investment in the future.

Another process developed more recently by Terry Walling is the Refocusing Network. Similar to the CCC, the RFN brings together four to 12 church leaders on a monthly basis under the guidance of a facilitator who has attended the RFN training. Walling states that the intent of the RFN is "to focus on [leaders'] personal development and the refocusing of their churches toward intentional mission ministry."

Walling has developed three different networks, which, when combined, form a comprehensive strategy for church revitalization. The three networks are: 1) Refocusing Leaders Networks, 2) Refocusing Churches Networks and 3) Mission-Focused Church Networks. Each network clusters the pastors and key leaders monthly for about one year. The first emphasizes the development of the leader as the crucial starting point to refocus a church. The second emphasizes strategic planning and vision development. The third emphasizes mission implementation and change.

Carefully developed material provides a guide by which the facilitator leads the participants through the various dimensions of each network. The advantage to this program is that it allows a district to send up to four persons to a two-day event where they will be trained as RFN facilitators. Your own trained people can then lead participants through each network process. There is an initial training cost for four individuals. Subsequently there is a fee for becoming a RFN facilitator and an annual renewal.

A third program that could meet the goals of a Strategic Planning Network is the New Beginnings program developed by Charles Arn of Church Growth, Inc. The program has been pilot tested and is finding good success.

This program is a comprehensive strategy designed to involve the total church in the process of revitalization. The method is through 1) a commitment to start an alternative congregation — worship-style or language — to reach a new constituency in the community; and 2) a commitment to begin at least three new ministry groups focused on three target groups.

Participation in the New Beginnings program extends for 12 months. It includes two major "conferences" or encounters with the program director and other participating churches. A final assessment of the intervention steps is conducted at the end of the 12-month period.

For many years I approached the work of district oversight carefully measuring the number of cases I took on so as not to overburden myself. When someone would ask, "What can be done about church X?" I would often say, "Well, I know I need to deal with it, but not this year. I can't open a can of worms if I'm unable to deal completely with it" — as if I were the only one who had the ability to help a struggling or plateaued church. Pretty arrogant, isn't it?

Well, in all reality I think overseers, who often have fairly strong egos, tend to like this indispensable role they create for themselves. But what about mission? Are they really doing what is the most effective in "Making Him Known"? In fact an overseer who holds selfishly to the position of savior of every struggling church actually limits his or her district growth.

Refocusing can happen only as fast and as frequently as he or she can effect it — one at a time. Why not release groups of people, equip and empower them to assist one another in a controlled, well-guided system of restoring health and vitality?

Harvest 1000

*Provide opportunity for focused emphasis on
church plants through development of a
supplemental financial network of regional lay leaders.*

Every district has some form of financial connection through which ministry efforts are funded. These district ministries may include overseer's support, leadership screening and development, office overhead, Christian education, camping, audits, missions, social action and many other possible activities. The funding system for this district ministry usually draws income from local churches on the premise that "together we can do what we can't do alone." The benefits of district connection are invaluable to the local church. The mature church understands that value even though it may not reap a proportional amount of benefits for its investment.

Church planting is clearly a regional ministry that can be effectively accomplished only by a group of churches pulling together. Even with this corporate commitment, however, funding is often the problem. Two factors are always at work in the district that make funding the church planting enterprise difficult.

1. The natural tendency of any institution is toward institutionalization and self-preservation. Additionally, there is the irrefutable need to provide for basic, non-negotiable in the district — overseer's support, audit fees, postage, telephone, rent, utilities and so forth. During financial constriction, which seems to be the norm rather than the exception, these "hard" costs are the last to be adjusted. The "soft" costs are easy prey to budget balancing efforts. CE, missions, social action, evangelism often pay the price for a bal-

anced budget and a healthy contingency reserve fund. Sodalic leader, don't fret. It's okay. We need everyone and everything. Don't think you can throw out the audit line item so you can plant a new church. You need basic operational overhead to build your district. Just make sure it's appropriate and not inflated.

Any serious church planting enterprise will require a budget line item of significant size. It will probably be the largest of the "soft" costs. As such it is a big target to hit when adjusting for a balanced budget. When that temptation comes, try to view the entire budget holistically. Further, ensure that your budget is consistent with your priorities. By looking at your budget could I tell you what's important to your district?

2. A second and related mitigating factor in funding the district church planting enterprise is the fact that it deals not with what is but what may be. Much of your planting budget is not yet tied to actual people or places. It's futures money. Most people in the church don't want to take a risk on a possibility if it may threaten what is reality. It's easy to reappropriate these dollars to real people, offices and expenses that we have now. The rationale goes, "No one will be hurt since there's no one 'out there' yet."

No one is hurt, or so we think. Actually, everyone is hurt as the future life of the district is slowly siphoned into the present black hole of self preservation. The extreme of this attitude says, "We shouldn't be planting new churches when there are so many struggling churches all around us." Let me give you a little clue. There's nothing that will renew the life of a district more than a few successful church plants. Every existing church in that district will be positively affected by a new church and the growth possibilities it represents.

Have you ever seen the face of a senior adult when you put a baby nearby? A smile, enthusiasm and new excitement are the result.

Removing or curtailing funds for church planting would be tantamount to Chrysler Corporation closing down its Research and Development department and telling us they'll stay with the K-cars. The result? Slowdown, shrinkage, stagnation and closing.

Fund your church planting efforts, whatever you do. It's your future, to say nothing of the best stewardship of your finances in fulfilling the Great Commission. Planting should have a significant presence in the general operational budget of the district. Yet this may not be enough to fund a truly aggressive system. Enter Harvest 1000 as a supplemental source with multiple objectives.

Objective one. Harvest 1000 raises funds designated for the church planting efforts in your district in general or for a specific planting project. It is clearly positioned as supplemental to the general operating budget. As such it must be clear that giving to church planting through Harvest 1000 is "over and above" personal tithing or corporate responsibility to the district. It provides a vehicle through which individual donors or churches may give specially to plant churches.

Objective two. Harvest 1000 provides an opportunity to network individuals with the interest and ability to make significant financial gifts. Although you will need to determine what "significant" means for your area and constituency, generally these people are financially capable beyond regular tithing. Often they even find themselves in somewhat of a vacuum and possibly a bit lonely. Perhaps they are the wealthiest persons in their church. They've had to learn to live with that role and the companionship of people in similar circumstances is welcome. Remember also that there is a good reason for their financial well-being. This kind of person has a success mentality and is probably somewhat aggressive if not intimidating. An opportunity to be with like-minded people and forge new and possibly lasting relationships is probably most welcome. Especially if there is the additional commonality of faith in Christ, denominational affiliation and proximity in the district. Who knows, two physicians or two attorneys or two business persons from two different churches may develop a friendship that will grow over a lifetime of involvement at camp, district meetings and business associations. What better place for such networking than within the church around the centerpiece of church planting.

Objective three. This is somewhat related to the second objective but broader. In most denominations there is a generation of strong lay leaders who have not only made significant financial investments over their lifetime but also served capably as influencers and leaders. There is a strength that has come from their presence. There is the financial stability and wisdom that they have provided. Yet they are aging. They probably became networked in the developing years of the denomination or district when moving into such institutional places of influence was expected. As these capable, spiritual men and women of God retire or join our Lord, a vacuum will be left unless we intentionally move to fill it. In today's pragmatic, movement-oriented society its not automatic that a new generation of financial- and leadership-minded lay persons will automatically gravitate to denominational or district involvement. The institution is no longer enough.

There must be a cause, a banner, a goal that is success-oriented and mission-driven. Harvest 1000 is all of the above. It is pragmatic, growth-oriented, mission-driven, faith-driven, aggressive and proactive. It provides the opportunity for a new generation of influencers to move into a common role of affecting the denomination for years to come with stability, leadership and wisdom. And here's the beauty of it all. Because this generation has been nurtured into their influential roles in the denomination or district through church planting, it will saturate their influence in everything else they do. Can you see how exciting the future of the church really can be? Imagine the new cadre of leaders, financial givers and key influencers all infected with the church planting bug. It will impact decisions made in budget committees, strategy meetings, organizational meetings, governing boards and task forces for 20 or 30 years.

The Harvest 1000 process is actually quite simple and straightforward. By the time you have a need for such an emphasis you will probably have someone in the district who is giving a fair amount of time to the system. These events will mostly become a coordination effort on their part.

A steering committee should be formed comprised of key individuals who will carry momentum and credibility to the participants. These should be people who will make their own contribution and can give you advice regarding the nature of such a fund raising event. Keep your committee to six or eight persons and empower your coordinator to take leadership in the meeting. What you want is their advice, so go with a fairly well-developed plan in mind.

Select dates and places for an evening program near the various churches in the district. Perhaps it will be a nice banquet facility, a hotel or restaurant. It must be conducive for a program. Let your advisors tell you their preference. Each event should cluster a small group of people from the surrounding churches. Smaller, intimate groups are more successful than large, massive events.

Line up a sharp, tight, well-planned program for each event that will include a brief statement of vision by the overseer, a brief explanation of the planting strategy by the appropriate person, the highlights of two or three projects set to begin (including the needs), testimony from a successful planter and a new Christian from a plant, quality music, a clear outline of how they can give — cash, pledge, deferred giving, an explanation of where they can give — specific plant, general planting, endowment fund; an invitation to leave personal information on the form.

They may choose to give that evening or later. They may want more information. They may want to talk personally with the planting coordinator or overseer. They may want someone to help them with a deferred gift in their estate. Whatever the option, provide it. Give them the freedom to give.

Be ready to follow up on their information. A visit, planned-giving help, information, whatever. Be ready. They'll expect it to be sharp and user-friendly. Your coordinator will need to think through carefully all of these items and prepare for them. Include your advisors as a primary source of help and guidance.

After each event, send the participants a list of those in attendance including their vocation. They will appreciate this networking. Plan to send out an update newsletter to keep the people informed regarding the planting progress of the district. Follow up through the coordinator, advisor or other appropriate person on any request made by a participant. Mobilize your resources to help them give.

Have attractive publications available to give to each participant. Provide personal invitations and quality follow-up pieces. This material and the event itself will cost a bit. Pay for it out of your budget, the proceeds of the event, or by gifts from your steering committee. Remember, it takes dollars to make dollars. Don't skimp but don't be irresponsible either.

Now, the question that's been banging around in your mind, "How do I identify prospective participants?" You may have a list in your head already. Even if you do, be sure the local pastors are fully aware and involved in what you're doing. I'd suggest taking the time to educate the pastors with the overall system strategy and get their emotional support. Then contact them requesting a list of people in their churches whom they believe have an interest and ability to support church planting above their tithe. Gain the confidence and support of the pastors. Some of them may be skittish about letting the district request direct financial support. You need to help them understand that in the long run this will probably enhance the leadership and support of that person in the local church. These are people who are motivated by the big picture and broader involvement. Harvest 1000 will serve to strengthen their commitment and enthusiasm locally.

Meta-Church Network

Clusters pastors of churches committed to understanding and implementing meta-church principles through equipping, study and diagnosis according to a prescribed curriculum.

You are probably familiar with the meta-church concepts presented by Carl George in his book *Prepare Your Church for the Future*. Perhaps you or some of the pastors in your district have attended Fuller Institute's "Beyond 800" seminar in which meta principles are taught. If not, I'd strongly suggest you familiarize yourself with this information. More and more pastors are adopting the meta-church model and leading their churches in its implementation.

The word *meta* simply means "change." At first glance some people think the word only describes the size of a church after it has passed the mega-church stage. In actuality the meta model has little to do with size and everything to do with philosophy and paradigm of ministry.

Churches of virtually all sizes may become meta churches. Don't make the mistake of thinking it is a program that can be implemented by board action. Meta-church thinking is an attitude that must become ingrained in the mind and habits of church leadership. It addresses governance, celebration events, small groups, support groups and outreach ministries of the local church. It is depicted in a coded "Meta-Globe," which requires proportional balance for health.

At its lowest denominator, "meta" is a ministry mind that reproduces leaders of tens. Obviously this is terribly simplistic and does little justice to the complex lifestyle of a truly meta church. I urge you to develop a basic knowledge of the meta model through George's book.

The principles on which the meta model is built have been around since the New Testament and are obvious in the Methodist movement of the 18th century. Churches today are rediscovering these timeless truths and being renewed and expanded through the meta mind set.

As you begin to understand the meta model through reading or seminar, be careful not to rush into implementation prematurely. Because it is an attitude not a program it must saturate your thinking and permeate key leadership. The natural result will be a new or changed approach to relevant, needs-based ministry.

It's at this point that the Meta-Church Network (MCN) is of such great help. The MCN allows a group of pastors to meet regularly under the guidance of a facilitator experienced in the implementation of meta ministry. The MCN will not only provide guidance to interested pastors, it may also forestall the pitfalls associated with overaggressive and premature application.

The MCN idea was conceived a few years ago in discussion with Pastor Steve Fitch. Steve's church in Rancho Cucamonga, CA, had been a pilot testing ground for Carl George's thinking. Steve and I were discussing the experience. I was anxious to resource a group of my key pastors with the material even though their churches hadn't quite reached the 800 mark.

The result of our conversation was a monthly meeting of pastors whom I had clustered and in whom I was anxious to invest. While Steve was able to moderate our discussions of the material with some technical experience, I was able to provide regular assurance and environment for these progressive pastors to exercise their creativity confidently and to push the limits of traditional expectations.

After a year of this kind of informal dialogue it was time to formalize the process. The group had developed a strong bond. Further, it was clear to them that the "establishment" (me) was not threatened by their interest but rather encouraged it.

Fitch began to develop systematic material in consultation with Carl George. While the nature of the group remained highly relational, the focus intensified on meta-church application. The material for the MCN, then, is an ongoing process of applying the meta model. It serves as a pragmatic complement to George's work. The material prepared by Fitch is being fully integrated into the strategy developed at Fuller Institute.

The MCN requires a commitment from three to five senior pastors who are intent on understanding the meta model. They must be prepared to assist in evaluating other MCN churches and to allow their churches to be thoroughly assessed by the group. Each network meeting is held on site at a different participating church. When a particular church is host, that pastor benefits from the group's objective insight regarding meta-church application. This requires advance diagnosis and description of the church by the pastor. Fuller Institute's "Data MIRROR" baseline and subscription is invaluable at this point. On a regular basis this service evaluates the local church progress in meta-model application. Further, George has developed modular tape seminars that can be applied as appropriate to the particular condition of the participating church.

Concurrent with this continuous, hands-on evaluation, the MCN curriculum provides systematic insight into the elements of the meta model. This dialogic emphasis combined with the practical exercise of first-hand evaluation provides a highly effective learning experience that will increase a senior pastor's proficiency.

"Now," you say, "how does the MCN fit in to a church planting system?" Well, do you remember how the effectiveness of the Pastor Factory increased in a cell-based church? Do you remember how important the paradigm of reproducing groups is to the Century 21 System? Do you remember the significance of being "staff-led and lay-ministry driven"? All of these principles and more are integral to the MCN. MCN churches will be the ones most likely to reproduce themselves. It's a good thing because churches with a meta mind are the ones you will most want to start. Because like begets like, you will see new churches begin with meta thinking from their inception.

CHAPTER 6 –
IMPLEMENTATION

By now your mind is filled with all sorts of questions: "How do we implement?" "How long does it take?" "How much does it cost?" Obviously I can't give you precise answers to those questions for your particular circumstance. I can, however, give some information in the form of estimates and examples that might be helpful.

Because it may take as long as five years to implement a total system, don't think you can begin a component tomorrow. A great deal of work must be done simply to set the environment and focus of the district leaders before even the first component can begin. General unity in commitment to planting must pervade district thinking. The pastoral team must be up to speed with the overseer's priority. Obviously some church planting activity will help to achieve this. Therefore, I would strongly urge you to put on a shotgun attitude as you begin. (see chapter 3) It's okay to start at the shotgun level and use outside resources to help move you toward a system. Let your district plant churches for now. The paradigm shift to churches planting churches will come later. Send your candidates somewhere else to be assessed for now. Your PAS will come. You see, even though you start the process in the shotgun phase you can begin the planning and training to ease you into the system phase. By so doing you can avoid many of the painful failures and flops some of us have endured in the process of learning.

Recently while working with a group of leaders in a small district in British Columbia it became evident that the environment was well-established to begin planting churches. The district could not, however, begin its components quickly. Our first assumption, then, was to begin in the shotgun phase while putting in place the events and training that would lead to a basic system in 18-24 months. In this plan, the district would seek candidates elsewhere, assess them elsewhere and, in order to get moving the district resources would focus directly on two plants. At the same time partnering with two other denominations would begin in order to start a Profile Assessment System and a New Church Incubator.

Even though you may begin in the shotgun phase, give careful attention to the preliminary steps of a system. This balance will prevent the problems between shotgun and system described in chapter 2 from becoming reality. If they do occur the result may be great pain and frustration. Don't underestimate the need to begin planning immediately for a basic system.

Much of the content of this chapter, especially the charts and graphs, has been fleshed out by Steve Fitch, who serves in the role of director in our district. His title is assistant superintendent for church planting. In that capacity he has mobilized a team of two others who work for him to maintain the total church planting system. In directing our planting enterprise he is an invaluable extension of my vision and ministry. As you read on you will begin to understand the significance of someone filling this role.

Let me begin with demonstrating how the system will work for you in a real-life case. In Appendix A you will find one church's plan to parent in a nearby city. It will help you see how the Century 21 System can help a local church fulfill its vision to reproduce itself. It provides insight from the local church perspective.

The following chart (Figure 8) allows you to see progression from one component to the next. The chart assumes a commitment by the local church to be a parent. This is either the result of the Strategic Planning

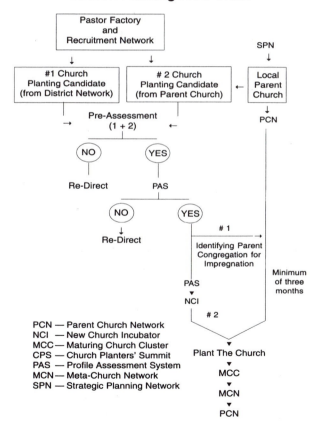

Century 21
Church Planting Flow Chart

Figure 8

Network, or it comes from a desire to reproduce, which is already present in the church.

Notice the two sources from which planter candidates may come. Number 1 is a candidate identified from some source other than the parent church. At least three months prior to the new church birth, this candidate should be placed within the parent church for a gestation period. This allows for ownership to build, support networks to form and emotional connections to be made. This will be a vital lifeline for the planter in the early stages of life.

Number 2 is the candidate who comes from within the parent church. This is ideal because the process of adjustment and bonding to the parent church has already occurred. The potentially stressful times of birthing are not compounded by the additional strain of building a new relationship with the planter. Both #1 and #2 candidates are the result of the influence of the Pastor Factory or Recruitment Network, which causes the pastor and/or overseer to consider him or her as a possible candidate.

While alternative congregations planted on-site may find planting candidates from the #1 source, increasingly the #2 source should quickly become the larger source of candidates for any new church — on- or off-site. Local parent churches should begin to produce their own planters. If this does not occur in time, it's a good indication that some key paradigm shifts have not occurred.

Don't assume you can have this entire system up and running overnight. From the time district leadership begins to consider the idea to full operational status might be a few years. Even implementing the three primary components (PCN, PAS and NCI) will require a year or more. Be patient but persistent. Time invested up front to develop mission, leadership and philosophy will be well spent. Don't short those. They'll pay high dividends during implementation.

Much of the work of implementation will be made easier by the early work of creating environment. This is primarily the responsibility of the overseer. District pastors and leaders must begin to see, understand and accept the overseer's commitment to planting. The overseer must use every chance to influence, not ramrod, just influence. Let's say it takes 3 - 6 months for the overseer to come to a personal commitment to plant churches (see chapter 2). Add another 12-18 months after that for the overseer to create a fertile environment through influencing pastors, lay leaders, boards and committees. Already you see that as much as two years might be spent simply doing the unseen spade work of preparing the soil and creating the environment. That's before any specific component is even implemented. Yet if the environment is right, implementation will be a breeze.

So, district overseer, you need to make a multiyear commitment. If you start it and leave the scene too early, the whole thing will cave in. That could be worse for the district than never having started at all. Once you make the commitment, see it through to the system phase.

Now obviously some districts will already have a significant amount of movement. The environment may be just right. Pastors and lay leaders are united in commitment to mission. There is anticipation and willingness to take steps forward in mission. Overseers along with key advisors and consultants will need to assess the level of development for their district case. The appropriate commitment may be to immediate church planting in the shotgun phase with deployment of the first system component within 6 months. Perhaps the district is ready for immediate system development. Whatever the case, carefully and prayerfully assess the district. Use your consultant, neighboring overseers, advisors, anyone who can help you make wise and appropriate decisions. And, remember, just as every church is different (see SPN) so also each district is different.

The following timeline (Figure 9) provides an example of how you might consider implementing the system in your area. This is based on the plan used in our own district. You may need to adjust or extend it for your circumstances. The leadership team referred to in the first step refers to three individuals charged with implementing the system. One is an assistant to the superintendent for planting. The other two support him or her.

In this case the shotgun phase actually lasted nearly five years. During that time many of the difficult circumstances resulted, to which I've alluded earlier. The process of creating an environment for a church planting movement took nearly three years. These are both extended periods because we were really feeling our way to find a systems approach. I hope our experience will benefit you. These can realistically be fulfilled in 18-24 months.

Century 21 System
Implementation Timeline

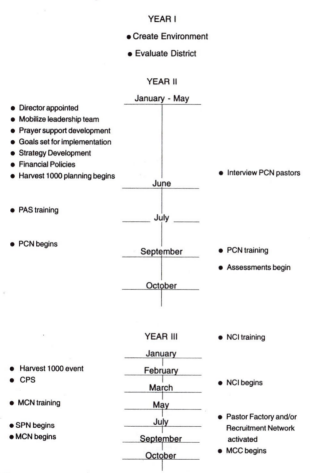

Figure 9

In addition to beginning each of the components over a designated time line, you will need to be aware of the general dynamics throughout the implementation process. There are four to be concerned about.

1. Philosophy Development involves the ongoing growth of the district in understanding the church planting movement as a system. (see chapter 3)

2. Leadership Development not only deals with the district overseer as described in chapter 2 but with the roles of director, facilitators and coaches described in chapter 4. This area requires not only identifying people for these roles but constant growth in their commitment to a church planting system.

3. Finance Development may require special attention. In providing the supplemental finances required for increased planting, paradigms of funding may need to shift. The governing boards may need to commit to church planting as a priority. Additionally they may need to adopt a philosophy of funding that will allow for special fund-raising efforts among district constituents for church planting. That will take time and attention.

4. Component Development is the process of training and starting the actual components that comprise the total system.

The following three charts (Figures 10, 11 and 12) developed by Fitch integrate these four dynamic areas with the previous implementation timeline. The goal is to keep each of these dynamic areas at similar levels of development within the implementation process.

Century 21 System Integrated Timeline

Dynamic Areas	Year 1											
	1st Qtr.			2nd Qtr.			3rd Qtr.			4th Qtr.		
	1	2	3	1	2	3	1	2	3	1	2	3
Philosophy Development	Create Environment			Evaluate District						Articulate New Strategy		
Leadership Development	Overseer Commitment Development			Evaluate Pastors			Begin Director Search			Begin Team Development		
Finance Development										Budget Adjusted for Strategy Launch		
Component Development							Develop Working Knowledge					

Figure 10

Century 21 System Integrated Timeline

Year 2

Dynamic Areas	1st Qtr.	2nd Qtr.	3rd Qtr.	4th Qtr.
Philosophy Development	Strategy Refinement			
Leadership Development	Director Appointed	Team Mobilized Prayer Support Active Interview PCN Pastors	Select Facilitators, Coaches, Assessors	
Finance Development		Develop Policies Harvest 1000 Planning	Policies Set	
Component Development	Implementation Goals Set		PAS Training PCN Training Assessments Begin	PCN Begins

Figure 11

Century 21 System Integrated Timeline

Year 3

Dynamic Areas	1st Qtr.			2nd Qtr.			3rd Qtr.			4th Qtr.		
	1	2	3	1	2	3	1	2	3	1	2	3
Philosophy Development		Highlight Progress										
Leadership Development		Select Facilitators, Coaches, Assessors										
Finance Development		Harvest 1000 Event										
Component Development		NCI Training CPS Retreat		NCI Begins MCN Training PAS Retraining			MCN Begins Pastor Factory and/or Recruitment Network Activated			MCC Begins SPN Begins		

Figure 12

Costs for implementing the components will vary from one to another. Some have predictable costs for training, purchase of ongoing curriculum and consulting. Others will be largely dependent on the specific decisions of the district. What follows is an attempt to identify the financial and personnel requirements for the first three components. This is by no means exhaustive and should not be considered authoritative for your situation. I simply want to help you consider the realistic costs for these components. Actual figures will be part of your own planning.

I do not include this information about the other seven for two reasons. Some of the curriculum is in final stages of development so costs are as yet not finalized. Secondly, selected components are so dependent on the individual district application that it's not possible to accurately estimate financial costs.

1. The Parent Church Network will require you to identify at least one facilitator and enough coaches for the number of churches planning to participate. So, for example, if you expect five churches in your PCN you will need one facilitator and five coaches.

Some coaches may be able to work with more than one church. Care should be taken not to overburden the coaches. A PCN should range in size from three to seven churches. Assuming a pastor and two lay leaders per church, this means a monthly network meeting of nine to 21 persons — a good range. Obviously, if you have more than seven churches interested in participating in a PCN, a second should be started. When attempting to identify the facilitator for the second PCN, the coaches in the first PCN will be your primary candidates.

The district overseer, designated facilitator and coaches should attend the PCN training scheduled by Church Resource Ministries throughout the country. The monetary cost for this training is still being finalized. Once you commit to begin a PCN, there will be a cost for the curriculum and continuing phone consultation. Additional training at subsequent PCN training events should also be considered.

2. The Profile Assessment System does not involve curriculum but does require intense training of the assessors.

You will need to select nine to 15 prospective assessors who will be trained by Dr. Charles Ridley. Keep in mind that these may be from more than one district or denomination but should be in the same general geographic area for easy accessibility. Be sure to identify one person to serve as logistical coordinator in scheduling assessments, contacting assessors and forwarding assessments to the proper persons.

Cost for the training event will be approximately $3,000. Variables that may affect the cost include travel for Dr. Ridley, cost of personality profiles on assessors, facilities used and whether a fish-bowl assessment is performed. This is your training event scheduled on your turf for your people. You have significant control over some of the expenses.

3. Costs for the New Church Incubator have been well-publicized in the past few years. Here again you will need to identify one facilitator for each NCI and provide one coach for each planter who participates. These should be the people, along with the overseer, who attend the NCI training.

The NCI training expense is approximately $750 plus travel for a team of five. Participation in the NCI includes curriculum and periodic coaching by Church Resource Ministries. This participation costs approximately $1200 with subsequent attendance at training events costing $150.

The costs for actually beginning a new church will also vary greatly depending on community, culture, denominational procedures and district history. Most groups have some type of assistance on a denominational and district level. With this in mind and assuming a tent-making approach by the planter, there are five funding sources that may be coordinated in the effort. The tent-making source might be defined in a number of ways. Perhaps the planter will hold a part-time secular job. It may be that the planter's spouse will provide this supplemental income. Maybe it's family members or close friends. In any case it's from some source other than the other four. It is related directly and personally to the church planter.

What follows is a chart identifying the five potential funding sources and tying specific expenses to those sources. This is an example only. Your plan may differ based on district or denominational circumstances. Actual dollar amounts are also for illustrative purposes and may vary in your case. Use a consultant or advisor with experience to help establish appropriate and realistic figures.

Funding Proposal for New Church Plants
Funding Sources
1) The District
2) Tent-Making Church Planters
3) Parent Churches
4) The Church Planting Core
5) The Denomination

Church Planting Expenses	Funded By
1) Pre-Planting Cost: (Assessments, Relocation)	#1
2) Benefits (Health Insurance & Pension)	#1 + #4
3) Supplemental Salary (1st yr $500/mo)	#1
(2nd yr $250/mo)	#1
4) Base Salary ($2000/mo for 2 yrs)	#2 + #3
5) Overhead Start-up Cost ($5000)	#1 + #3
6) Ongoing Overhead Cost	#4
7) Major Milestone Assistance (First Building Lease and Purchase)	#1 + #5

Assuming the level of financial support established in the previous chart, assuming two new church plants per year and assuming a two-year financial commitment, your district commitment would look like the following chart. Remember that these are figures for actual church planting costs. Your district budget will include expenses for other items, such things as training, system development, staff and so forth. So don't think that this represents the total amount your district should budget for the church planting enterprise. You might divide your budget into three categories. 1) Personnel — a paid person to direct and oversee the system; 2) system — costs outlined earlier for component training and implementation; and 3) church plants — money going directly to assist individual plants as explained above. The chart outlines (Figure 13) the third of these budget categories.

Two-Year District Commitment

Category	Year 1	Year 2
1st Project	$ 19,000	$ 7,000
2nd Project	19,000	7,000
Start-up 1st	5,000	0
Start-up 2nd	5,000	0
Total 1st year	$ 48,000	$ 14,000
3rd Project		$ 19,000
4th Project		19,000
Start-up 3rd		5,000
Start-up 4th		5,000
Total 1st year		$ 48,000
Total 2nd year		$ 62,000

Figure 13

In order for you to understand the full financial magnitude of beginning one new church, you might chart the costs and funding sources together. The Comprehensive Support Charts that follow provide examples. They show the costs for starting one off-site plant (Figure 14a) and one on-site plant (Figure 14b). Notice that the on-site costs are less. This is due to the fact that start up overhead costs are minimal. You already have the building, office, equipment and so forth. Remember that starting alternate congregations is a viable way to plant churches.

A. Off-Site Church Plants

Comprehensive Support Chart

	District	Parent Church	Planter	Core Families	Category Total
1ST YEAR					
Salary	$ 6,000	$ 12,000	$ 12,000		$ 30,000
Insurance/Pension*	8,000				8,000
Start-up	5,000	5,000			10,000
Operating				$ 16,000	16,000
1ST YEAR TOTALS	$ 19,000	$ 17,000	$ 12,000	$ 16,000	$ 64,000
2ND YEAR					
Salary	$ 3,000	$ 6,000	$ 12,000	$ 9,000	$ 30,000
Insurance/Pension*	4,000			4,000	8,000
Start-up					
Operating				32,000	32,000
2ND YEAR TOTALS	7,000	6,000	12,000	45,000	70,000
GRAND TOTALS	$ 26,000	$ 23,000	$ 24,000	$61,000	$ 134,000

* Depends on health and pension costs in your area or group.

Figure 14a

B. On-Site Church Plants

Comprehensive Support Chart

	District	Parent Church	Planter	Core Families	Category Total
<u>1ST YEAR</u>					
Salary	$ 6,000	$ 12,000	$ 12,000		$ 30,000
Insurance/Pension*	8,000				8,000
Start-up					
Operating		6,000			6,000
1ST YEAR TOTALS	$ 14,000	$ 18,000	$ 12,000		$ 44,000
<u>2ND YEAR</u>					
Salary	$ 3,000	$ 6,000	$ 12,000	$ 9,000	$ 30,000
Insurance/Pension*	4,000			4,000	8,000
Start-up					
Operating				6,000	6,000
2ND YEAR TOTALS	7,000	6,000	12,000	19,000	44,000
GRAND TOTALS	$ 21,000	$ 24,000	$ 24,000	$19,000	$ 88,000

* Depends on health and pension costs in your area or group.

Figure 14b

Again, these figures are for example only. Costs in your area may vary widely. Further, the financial responsibility shared by the planter and core families may fluctuate based on the readiness of the core to bear the load and the ability of the planter to be involved in tent-making. The important thing to note is the cooperation required between planter and core and the progressive shift of responsibility between the two.

Throughout the entire implementation process take advantage of your advisor or consultant. As addressed in chapter 2, this is a very important relationship to develop early in the process. It may be a partnering sodality (see chapter 3), a consultant, a denominational advisor, or a neighboring district leader. Objective, unbiased input on strategy and implementation will be invaluable to your efforts. In that role Bob Logan and Steve Ogne have kept us from some potentially disastrous results. Additionally, the role of the director as explained in chapter 5 may make or break the success and extent of the system development. If your district is unable to support a director of church planting, or if it is impossible to share one with neighboring districts, the speed and extent of implementation will be greatly reduced. In that capacity Steve Fitch has proved the significance of this role in implementing the Century 21 System for us.

Now, if you're anything like me, you've read many books that purport to help you in your ongoing effort to be an effective church leader. You read the last chapter on implementation and close the book with a lingering desire for more information and someone to walk with you in applying your new insights. You may even make a valiant effort to begin the implementation process. Yet with no accountability and no consistent coaching your effort wanes into oblivion.

I'd like to encourage you with the knowledge that the help and regular coaching of a network is in place to assist leaders to apply the concepts described in this book.

This book describes one district's experience and suggests that what occurred in one place can occur in many others. A pilot Century 21 System Network has formed to replicate the Century 21 System implementation process in a systematic way. Ultimately this will give rise to a network that provides guidance and accountability for district leaders in their own implementation process.

In your case, then, closing the book doesn't mean relegating the ideas to a low probability for implementation. It simply means you're ready seriously to consider stepping from phase I to phase II — from reading about it to making it work with the help of the Century 21 System Network.

CONCLUSION

I trust that by now you have experienced some inner "eureka" experience that will lead to freshness and renewed energy in your responsibilities within the district. Whether you are a district overseer, church growth leader, pastor or local lay leader you have a place in your district's future. The choice is yours as to what priorities you bring to your involvement.

You may want to go back and reread the chapter on Mission. It will bring your interest and investigation of church planting full circle. I am convinced that an unequivocal commitment to church planting as the primary mission-driven enterprise of your district will usher in renewal, which we all want but is so elusive.

There are a few secondary, but really primary, benefits from implementing the Century 21 Church Planting System. Obviously, the primary result is that churches are planted, souls are saved and lives are transformed by God. In the process, however, consider these.

1. Relationships within the district are formed and centered around the primary mission of the church — to make God known.

2. Many individuals become involved as participants. Therefore, the success and future of church planting is not dependent on one or two individuals. Rather it is part of the very fiber of the district.

3. Because one district may not have the ability to support its own system, the opportunity to work

jointly with other districts and denominations is optimum. The walls of sectarianism are broken. I do not support the oft-repeated statement that the church is moving into a post-denominational era. Conversely, more and more people, pastors and churches are asking for the kind of support, accountability and multigenerational stability available only through some type of denominational connection. We are, however, in an increasingly interdenominational era. As each group sees the Kingdom mission more clearly, we become more pragmatic in our methods, less obsessed with our differences and interested in cooperative Kingdom effort. Don't misunderstand; this is not to minimize denominational distinctives. Each is unique. That uniqueness should be developed. It's just that we are more and more able to accept one another as Kingdom partners and enjoy the richness that diversity brings to a common mission.

Through this book you may have picked up on a few major paradigm shifts that are required for successful implementation of the Century 21 Church Planting System. The issue I described in number three above is obviously one that affects the very identity of the church. There are six others that directly relate to this system. I want to state them briefly here to ensure that they have not slipped by unnoticed.

1. Churches plant churches. This represents a major shift of responsibility for church planting from the district to the local church. Churches reproduce themselves and districts provide the environment and resources for them to be successful. As I told my Parent Church pastors, "My commitment is to create an environment for you to be successful in reproducing your church. Your job is to do it."

This is perhaps the most difficult paradigm shift to make. It has to occur, however, for there to be success. It starts with the overseer and must include the primary church-growth leaders, a majority of the pastors and key local lay leaders. You're the ones for whom this book is written.

2. Production capacity is built. This requires that leadership put time, energy and money in developing systems to create the environment for church planting. The Century 21 System is inherently production capacity. It will cost to implement. Leaders must shift their resources from the front lines of planting one church at a time to the systems that will multiply churches.

3. Leadership is paramount. To repeat myself, the church rises and falls on leadership. District overseers must step forward proactively declaring mission, vision and the priority of church planting. They can no longer assume that their role is simply that of a management position. They can no longer call themselves administrators. They must be leaders.

4. Mission is central. Just as every wheel has a hub, the district must have a mission. Everything that is done must have a direct bearing on the mission. This shift may require the dismantling of some committees, elimination of some positions, creation of new positions and the start of activities. The district can no longer follow the path that creates the least turmoil or conflict. Conflict or not, it must be mission-driven.

5. Alternative congregations are church plants. Look around you and see the cultural and stylistic diversity of our culture. Beginning an alternative congregation as a ministry to a different group of people is tacitly planting a new church. We must allow the

church planting enterprise to include these options. Further, we must plan for this type of growth and prepare for it.

6. Build on strengths. Usually the Christian spirit motivates the corporate body to assist the hurting among us. Unfortunately this spirit carries over so strongly to district activity that we forget about the strengths, the hot spots, the blue chippers, the happening places. Shift the primary resources to build on these strengths. Not to the total exclusion of the struggling churches but strongly enough to let these growing churches, successful leaders and active groups become the engines that pull your district train. Allow these strengths to define the priorities and pace of your district. We don't want to exclude anyone, but neither do we want to move as slowly as the slowest ship. One of two extremes in any organization will define the expectations of its participants — the struggling or the healthy. Without intentional effort the struggling groups will determine the parameters. The paradigm shift must intentionally place emphasis on strengths as the defining criteria.

My prayer is that as you embark on a new emphasis in your life, church and district you will view it as a journey of joyful discovery. When you're not sure, trust the nudging of God's Spirit. He has given you abilities and a passion. Believe that He will guide you in all understanding as you obediently live out His call for you. I will pray for you — for courage, for confidence and for boldness in building the kingdom of our God and of His Christ.

God be with you.

APPENDIX A

The Menifee Plan

The Lamb's Fellowship, Temecula, CA

(Note: At least one year has been given to creating environment and vision casting prior to formal introduction of this plan.)

Phase One: Organize families from the parent church, the Lamb's Fellowship of Temecula, CA, who are currently living in Menifee, Sun City, Canyon Lake, Perris and Moreno Valley areas for the purpose of:

a. Offering small group ministries (home fellowships) to those attending the Temecula church, but who have been geographically distanced.

b. Create the opportunity strategically to evangelize those areas beyond the Temecula Valley.

c. Explore the potential and interest of planting a second Free Methodist church with the distinctive philosophy of ministry and style of the Lamb's Fellowship in Temecula. Other than the official board and pastor's cabinet, no mention of plans for a church plant will be made within the first quarter (10 weeks).

d. Begin participation in Parent Church Network.

e. Potential seed families may include: (names have been changed for illustration)

(From the general directory:)

01.	Bob & Carol Beggar	Menifee
02.	Tony Brown	Sun City
03.	Mike & Kathy Cat	Homeland
04.	Tommy Duncan	Menifee
05.	Rob & Eileen Ellis	Menifee
06.	Keith Franklin	Sun City
07.	Mark & Becky Gem	Sun City
08.	Bob & Alysha Frank	Sun City
09.	Mark & Lisa Hope	Menifee
10.	Darin & Sue Jenkins	Homeland
11.	Mark & Sheri Samo	Moreno
12.	Pat & Tina Simmons	Menifee
13.	Terry & Teresa Tune	Sun City
14.	Ralph & Sue Thompson	Sun City
15.	Pat Thompson	Sun City
16.	Randy & Linda Uke	Menifee
17.	Harry & Ruth Whelm	Perris
18.	Rachael Williamson	Sun City
19.	Sylvia Witherspoon	Sun City
20.	Randall Zimmerman	Menifee

f. Identify potential planter candidates from those within the congregation who have expressed a calling to ministry.

Phase Two: If one or more groups have demonstrated faithfulness and consistency throughout the first quarter, with an average combined attendance of 20 or more adults, three steps should then be taken to enter Phase Two;

a. Overseer is approached for his input and permission to present an official plan to the official board.

b. Input and permission to approach the seed families is sought from the official board.

c. Potential seed families are presented with the idea and an initial assessment of their interest is made. Five or more family units will need to express significant interest for the plan to continue on to Phase Three

d. Church planter is identified and is meeting district standards and requirements for ordination and church planting. That is, appropriate level of licensure is sought and assessment is performed by the Profile Assessment System.

Phase Three: Strategy to reach a core unit of no less than 50 committed adults begins.

a. Presentation is made to the Temecula congregation for the purpose of informing those who may be from the designated area and interested in participating in the new church plant.

b. Planter and spouse attend the Church Planters' Summit.

c. Planter begins participation in the New Church Incubator.

d. Menifee team escalates efforts to invite friends, family and neighbors to one of the area home fellowships. A third and fourth home fellowship is started if needed. Groups should not exceed 12-15.

e. New believers and transfers are temporarily assimilated into the Temecula church.

f. Monthly fellowship services are held in the Menifee area for the purpose of bonding and prayer.

g. The Menifee Covenant is made with all seed families.

"I commit my support to this new church by ..."
- ... agreeing to serve and attend for at least one year
- ... faithfully tithing my income
- ... serving in one major and one minor ministry area
- ... praying daily for the pastor and the ministry of my church

Phase Four: When a core unit of no less than 50 committed adults will be realized Phase Four is put into action;

a. Planter has secured a financial base with advice and approval of the Parent Church Network and according to district guidelines. This will include bi-vocational support, district support, parent church support and core group support.

b. Temecula begins to identify and provide items for Menifee start up.
- Advertising
- Furniture; chairs, tables, podium
- Nursery equipment
- Directional signs

- Sound system
- Literature

c. Temecula church provides administrative support
- Temporary office space and equipment for planter (6 mos.)
- Secretarial support (6 mos.)
- Temecula staff to work alongside Menifee volunteers

d. Temecula volunteers assist Menifee its first six Sundays.

e. Strategies for advertising are complete.

f. Facilities are located.

g. Date for first public service is set.

Phase Five: Having completed phases one through four, the Lamb's Fellowship of Temecula is now ready to give birth to the Lamb's Fellowship of Menifee.

a. Massive advertising blitz on target communities.

b. One hundred Temecula adults commit to Menifee's attendance for the first three weeks; moral support and frontline ministries. Allow Menifee's core to be in the services.

c. Fifty Temecula adults commit to an additional three weeks.

APPENDIX B

Component Contacts

As I've already mentioned, beginning the Century 21 Church Planting System will require implementation of one component at a time. There are different groups or individuals responsible for the development and replication of each component.

Imagine that you have 10 books by different authors. Each has been written independently by qualified experts in the field. The Century 21 System is the bookshelf that holds all 10 in a cohesive, orderly fashion. To access any one of the books you can make direct contact with its author/developer. The bookshelf can also give you guidance in your process.

Below is a list of contacts to help you get started. You are free to contact my office to point you in the right direction and provide advice, or you may go directly to the developer to begin your system.

1. Century 21 Church Planting System
   Dr. Kevin W. Mannoia
   Free Methodist Regional Ministries Center
   777 E. Alosta Ave., Azusa, CA 91702

2. Parent Church Network
   Dr. Robert Logan and/or Rev. Steve Ogne
   Church Resource Ministries
   PO Box 1354, Alta Loma, CA 91701
   (Note: Free Methodist groups should contact
   the Regional Ministries Center in Southern California)

3. Profile Assessment System
   Dr. Charles Ridley
   Indiana University, Wright Education Bldg.
   201 N. Rose Ave.,
   Bloomington, IN 47405-1006

or

   Dr. Robert Logan
   Church Resource Ministries
   PO Box 1354, Alta Loma, CA 91701

or

   Dr. Kevin W. Mannoia
   Free Methodist Regional Ministries Center
   777 E. Alosta Ave., Azusa, CA 91702

4. New Church Incubator
   Dr. Robert Logan and/or Rev. Steve Ogne
   Church Resource Ministries
   PO Box 1354, Alta Loma, CA 91701

5. Pastor Factory
   Rev. Neil Cole
   Church Resource Ministries
   5719 Beryl Street, Alta Loma, CA 91737

6. Church Planters' Summit
   Rev. Tweed Moore
   Free Methodist Regional Ministries Center
   777 E. Alosta Ave., Azusa, CA 91702

7. Maturing Church Cluster
   Contact Dr. Kevin W. Mannoia or
   Dr. Robert Logan for advice.

8. Strategic Planning Network
   Cluster Catalyzing Consultation
   Dr. Ray Ellis
   Free Methodist World Minstries Center
   PO Box 535002, Indianapolis, IN 46253-5002

or

Refocusing Network
Rev. Terry Walling
271 E. Imperial Way, Suite #621
Fullerton, CA 92635-1020

or

New Beginnings
Dr. Chip Arn
Church Growth, Inc. Box 541
Monrovia, CA 91017

9. Harvest 1000
Rev. Steve Fitch
Free Methodist Regional Ministries Center
777 E. Alosta Ave., Azusa, CA 91702

10. Meta-Church Network
Rev. Steve Fitch
Free Methodist Regional Ministries Center
777 E. Alosta Ave., Azusa, CA 91702